HODDER GCSE HISTORY FOR EDEXCEL

KU-542-552

EARLY ELIZABETHAN ENGLAND

1558–88

Barbara Mervyn

Acknowledgements

The Publishers would like to thank the following for permission to reproduce copyright material:

Photo credits

p. 2 © World History Archive/Alamy Stock Photo; **p. 9** © Keith Heron/Alamy Stock Photo; **p. 17** © GL Archive/Alamy Stock Photo; **p. 21** © The Print Collector/Alamy Stock Photo; **p. 27, p. 65** © ACTIVE MUSEUM/Alamy Stock Photo; **p. 36** © ACTIVE MUSEUM/Alamy Stock Photo; **p. 38** ©2005 TopFoto; p. 40 National Galleries Of Scotland/Hulton Fine Art Collection/Getty Images; **p. 42** © Pictorial Press Ltd / Alamy Stock Photo; **p. 43** © PAINTING/Alamy Stock Photo; **p. 46** © Archivart/Alamy Stock Photo; **p. 48** © World History Archive/Alamy Stock Photo; **p. 55, p. 56** © World History Archive/Alamy Stock Photo; **p. 60** *l* Bates Littlehales/National Geographic/Getty Images; **p. 60** *r*, **p. 72** © Hulton Archive/Stringer/Getty images; **p. 62** © The Granger Collection/TopFoto; **p. 69** © North Wind Picture Archives/Alamy Stock Photo; **p. 71** De Agostini Picture Library/Getty Images; **p. 73** *l*, **p. 101** © Lebrecht Music and Arts Photo Library/Alamy Stock Photo; **p. 73** *tr* © De Agostini Picture Library/Getty Images; **p. 73** *br* © Lebrecht Music and Arts Photo Library/Alamy Stock Photo; **p. 80** © Glenn Beanland/Lonely Planet Images/Getty Images; **p. 81** © Images of Birmingham/Alamy Stock Photo; **p. 82** *tl* © Mary Evans Picture Library/Alamy Stock Photo; **p. 82** *tr* © Mary Evans Picture Library/Alamy Stock Photo; **p. 82** *b* © Mary Evans Picture Library / Alamy; **p. 83** *tl* © Mary Evans Picture Library/Alamy Stock Photo; **p. 83** *ml* © Mary Evans Picture Library/Alamy; **p. 83** *bl* © Granger, NYC./Alamy Stock Photo; **p. 83** *tr* © Bridgeman Images/TopFoto; **p. 83** *br* © Hulton Archive/GettyImages; **p. 85** *t* Geraint Lewis/REX/Shutterstock; **p. 85** *b* Photographer Times Newspapers/REX/Shutterstock; **p. 86** *m* © Peter Brown/Alamy Stock Photo; **p. 86–87** Luis Davilla/Moment Mobile/Getty Images; **p. 88** © Leemage/Universal Images Group/GettyImages; **p. 93** © Christer Fredriksson/Lonely Planet Images/GettyImages; **p. 99** Francis Drake (c.1540-96) in the New World (engraving) (b/w photo), English School, (16th century) / Private Collection/Bridgeman Images; **p. 102** © Hi-Story/Alamy Stock Photo; **p. 103** © Dea/G. Dagli orti/De Agostini Picture Library/GettyImages; **p. 104** © Universal History Archive/Universal Images Group/GettyImages; **p. 108** Queen Elizabeth I (1538-1603) in Old Age, c.1610 (oil on panel), English School, (17th century)/Corsham Court, Wiltshire / Bridgeman Images; **p. 111** Miramax/Laurie Sparham/Hulton Archive/Getty Images.

Acknowledgements

p. 26, p. 43, p. 44 *t*, **p. 110** *bl* C. Haigh, *Elizabeth I*, (Longman, 1998); **p. 44** *b* J. Neale, *Queen Elizabeth I* (Doubleday/Jonathan Cape, 1934); **p. 54** S. Alford, The Watchers: A Secret History of the Reign of Elizabeth I (Allen Lane, 2012); **p. 68** R. Hutchinson, *Elizabeth's Spymaster* (Thomas Dunne Books, 2007); **p. 70** *b*, **p. 72** *tr* F. Fernández-Armesto, *The Spanish Armada* (Oxford University Press, 1988); **p. 73** P. Hammer, *Elizabeth's Wars* (Palgrave Macmillan, 2003); **p. 110** *tl* S. Doran, 'A Look at the Myth and Reality of the Virgin Queen's Reign: Elizabeth I', *The Historian*, issue 54 (London Historical Association, 1997); **p. 110** *tr* J. Hurstfield, *The Elizabethan Nation* (Pelican, 1964); **p. 110** *br*, **p. 111** D. Loades, 'Elizabeth I: Golden Reign of Gloriana', (The National Archives, 2003).

Thanks to Andy Harmsworth for use of material from *Elizabethan England: a study in depth*, pages 10, 12, 13, 20, 28, 33, 35, 36, 37, 60, 68, 88, 89, 90, 91, 96–7, 99, 100.

Every effort has been made to trace all copyright holders, but if any have been inadvertently overlooked, the Publishers will be pleased to make the necessary arrangements at the first opportunity.

Orders: please contact Bookpoint Ltd, 130 Park Drive, Milton Park, Abingdon, Oxon OX14 4SE. Telephone: +44 (0)1235 827720. Fax: +44 (0)1235 400454. Email education@bookpoint.co.uk Lines are open from 9 a.m. to 5 p.m., Monday to Saturday, with a 24-hour message answering service. You can also order through our website: www.hoddereducation.co.uk

ISBN: 978 1 4718 6181 9

© Barbara Mervyn 2016

First published in 2016 by
Hodder Education,
An Hachette UK Company
Carmelite House
50 Victoria Embankment
London EC4Y 0DZ

www.hoddereducation.co.uk

Impression number   10 9 8 7 6 5 4 3 2

Year   2020 2019 2018 2017 2016

Cover photos *left* © Ann Ronan Pictures/Print Collector/Getty Images, *right* © The Print Collector/Corbis

Illustrations by Oxford Designers and Illustrators, and Peter Lubach.

Typeset in ITC Legacy Serif 10/12pt by DC Graphic Design Limited

Printed in Italy

A catalogue record for this title is available from the British Library.

CONTENTS

1.1 Introducing Elizabeth and her England

Elizabeth I is one of the most famous monarchs in English history. Some people have admired her so much they have called her 'Good Queen Bess', and even 'Gloriana' because she was so gloriously successful. Your GCSE course gives you the opportunity to study in depth the issues Elizabeth faced and decide whether she deserves such a successful reputation. This chapter introduces Elizabeth herself, the people and the events of this dramatic reign.

Elizabeth I was crowned Queen in January 1559, aged 25. Although she was the daughter of Henry VIII, she had not expected to rule. However, her brother, Edward, and older half-sister, Mary, both died without having children, so Elizabeth became Queen.

Mary's reign had been very unpopular. Epidemics of disease and poor harvests had caused many thousands of deaths. Religious changes had led to rebellion and executions. War with France had been a disaster. Therefore, when Mary died, people were cautious about their new monarch. Would another queen be another failure?

Elizabeth put on an extravagant coronation. She travelled on a barge along the river Thames. Then crowds lined the streets to watch Elizabeth, her lords and ladies approach Westminster Abbey. Elizabeth had four new dresses made for that one day alone. In Elizabeth's coronation portrait, you can see the richness of her coronation gown, with the white fur, ermine, symbolising purity. Elizabeth wore her hair loose because that represented virginity.

> Why was it important for Elizabeth to impress her people at her coronation? **?**

◀ Elizabeth's coronation portrait, issued by her government in 1559, the year of her coronation. This coronation scene is famous and has been copied in films made about Elizabeth, as you can see on page 42.

UNDERSTANDING ELIZABETHAN ENGLAND

To understand the actions and decisions of people during Elizabeth's reign, you need to understand sixteenth-century life and thinking. These questions will remind you of some of the main differences between then and now. (Answers can be found on page 125.)

1. Was the population in the middle of the sixteenth century:
   a) 3–4 million and mainly living in towns
   b) about 2.5 million and divided equally between towns and the countryside
   c) about 3 million and mainly living in the countryside?

2. What did most people do for a living?
   a) Worked for the government or the Church
   b) Worked on the land in farming
   c) Set up small businesses.

3. What was most important factor in deciding the cost of food?
   a) The government set food prices.
   b) Shop owners set food prices.
   c) The quality of the harvest.

4. Was the average life expectancy:
   a) about 35 years
   b) about 45 years
   c) about 70 years?

5. True or false?
   F a) Henry VIII had changed the country's religion from Protestant to Catholic.
   T b) Plague broke out regularly, especially in towns.
   T c) Most people had no knowledge of the Americas or Asia.
   T d) Death from starvation was a real danger if there were three or more bad harvests in succession.
   T e) Religious changes had led to several major protests and rebellions between 1534 and 1558.
   F f) Girls had the same educational opportunities as boys.
   T g) People believed their monarch was God's representative, so rebelling against the monarch was rebelling against God.
   h) As Queen, Elizabeth was responsible for deciding whether to declare war or make peace.
   i) Kings and queens left decisions about religion to their bishops.
   j) As Queen, Elizabeth was responsible for calling meetings of Parliament and deciding how long they lasted.

THE TUDOR DYNASTY

Elizabeth was the last of the Tudors – the **dynasty** of kings and queens who ruled England from 1485 to 1603. These boxes contain information about the reigns of Elizabeth's father, brother and half-sister.

List three things Elizabeth could learn from these earlier reigns that might help her as Queen.

Henry VIII, reigned 1509–47

Henry believed he needed a male heir, although he had a daughter, Mary. He made himself Head of the English Church, instead of the Pope, so he could divorce and re-marry. The Church remained Catholic but was more moderate and contained some Protestant influences. Religious change led to opposition, especially after Henry closed the monasteries. A major rebellion, the Pilgrimage of Grace, broke out in the north in 1536. Over 200 rebels were executed. Henry's wars with France and Scotland in the 1540s pushed up food prices and unemployment, so poverty increased.

Edward VI, reigned 1547–53

Under Edward, Henry's longed-for son, the Church of England became Protestant. Decoration was removed from churches and an English Prayer Book replaced the Latin version. In 1549, Catholics in the south-west rebelled, and 2,500 were killed by the royal army. Harvests were bad and prices rose, increasing poverty. Thousands of cloth-workers and farm labourers lost their jobs, causing a rebellion in Norfolk in 1549. The royal army killed 3,000 rebels. When Edward died young, without children, the Duke of Northumberland tried to make his daughter-in-law, Lady Jane Grey, Queen. However, even Protestants supported the Tudor heir, Mary, although she was Catholic.

Mary I, reigned 1553–58

Mary, the daughter of Henry VIII and Catherine of Aragon, was Catholic and married Philip II of Spain, also a Catholic. In 1554, Wyatt's Rebellion broke out because of fears that the Spanish would control the country. Mary defeated the rebellion and executed 90 rebels. Mary restored the authority of the Pope, and over 300 Protestants who refused to change their religion were executed. Severe epidemics of influenza killed many thousands. After two terrible harvests, prices rose sharply and people died of starvation. Mary also joined Spain in war against France, but lost Calais, which had been under English control for over 200 years.

1.2 A story of triumph and success?

The timeline below shows you the main events, the overall story of Elizabeth's reign. Your task is to use this timeline to begin thinking about whether Elizabeth was a success – did she really deserve the title 'Good Queen Bess'?

To decide whether Elizabeth was a success, we need criteria to help us. Here are four criteria – the things that were seen by people in the 1500s as evidence of a successful monarch. The criteria are in different colours because they link to the events on the timeline below.

Did she defend her country from foreign threats? (Or did she create those threats?)

Did she unite her people in one religion? (Or did she create greater religious divisions?)

Did she help her people live prosperously and enjoy their lives? (Or was there widespread poverty?)

Did she make sure she had a clear successor? (Or did she leave people afraid of civil war breaking out over the crown when she died?)

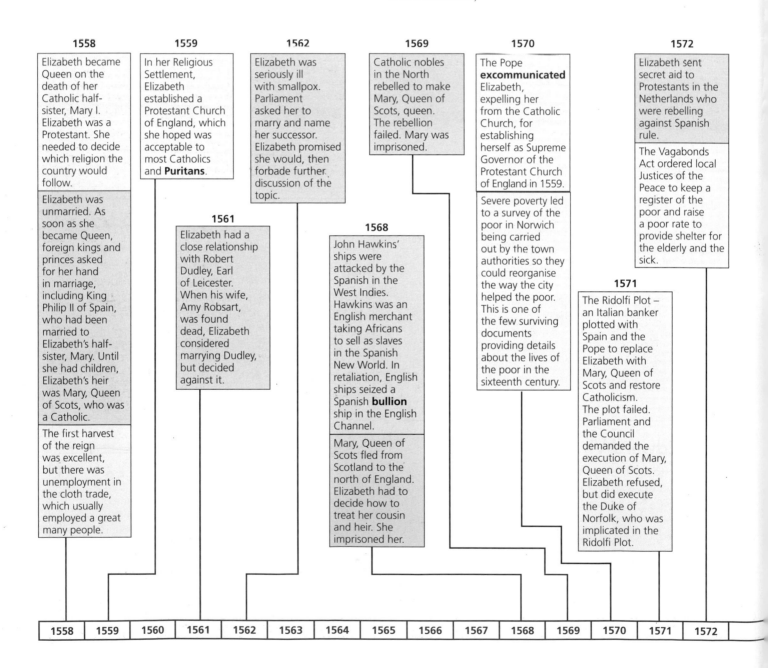

1558
Elizabeth became Queen on the death of her Catholic half-sister, Mary I. Elizabeth was a Protestant. She needed to decide which religion the country would follow.

Elizabeth was unmarried. As soon as she became Queen, foreign kings and princes asked for her hand in marriage, including King Philip II of Spain, who had been married to Elizabeth's half-sister, Mary. Until she had children, Elizabeth's heir was Mary, Queen of Scots, who was a Catholic.

The first harvest of the reign was excellent, but there was unemployment in the cloth trade, which usually employed a great many people.

1559
In her Religious Settlement, Elizabeth established a Protestant Church of England, which she hoped was acceptable to most Catholics and **Puritans**.

1561
Elizabeth had a close relationship with Robert Dudley, Earl of Leicester. When his wife, Amy Robsart, was found dead, Elizabeth considered marrying Dudley, but decided against it.

1562
Elizabeth was seriously ill with smallpox. Parliament asked her to marry and name her successor. Elizabeth promised she would, then forbade further discussion of the topic.

1568
John Hawkins' ships were attacked by the Spanish in the West Indies. Hawkins was an English merchant taking Africans to sell as slaves in the Spanish New World. In retaliation, English ships seized a Spanish **bullion** ship in the English Channel.

Mary, Queen of Scots fled from Scotland to the north of England. Elizabeth had to decide how to treat her cousin and heir. She imprisoned her.

1569
Catholic nobles in the North rebelled to make Mary, Queen of Scots, queen. The rebellion failed. Mary was imprisoned.

1570
The Pope **excommunicated** Elizabeth, expelling her from the Catholic Church, for establishing herself as Supreme Governor of the Protestant Church of England in 1559.

Severe poverty led to a survey of the poor in Norwich being carried out by the town authorities so they could reorganise the way the city helped the poor. This is one of the few surviving documents providing details about the lives of the poor in the sixteenth century.

1571
The Ridolfi Plot – an Italian banker plotted with Spain and the Pope to replace Elizabeth with Mary, Queen of Scots and restore Catholicism. The plot failed. Parliament and the Council demanded the execution of Mary, Queen of Scots. Elizabeth refused, but did execute the Duke of Norfolk, who was implicated in the Ridolfi Plot.

1572
Elizabeth sent secret aid to Protestants in the Netherlands who were rebelling against Spanish rule.

The Vagabonds Act ordered local Justices of the Peace to keep a register of the poor and raise a poor rate to provide shelter for the elderly and the sick.

1558	1559	1560	1561	1562	1563	1564	1565	1566	1567	1568	1569	1570	1571	1572

'GOOD QUEEN BESS'? – THE STORY IN OUTLINE

1. Look at each theme on the timeline in turn – their colour links them to the four success criteria listed on page 4. How successful do you think Elizabeth was in handling each theme? Choose from the following for each one:
   - ☐ She succeeded consistently.
   - ☐ She succeeded occasionally.
   - ☐ She failed.
   - ☐ I am not sure.

2. Choose two short periods of time that were particularly dangerous for Elizabeth and explain why you chose them.

3. Work with a partner. Your task is to tell the outline story of Elizabeth's reign from 1558 to 1588 in one minute – you can say a lot in one minute! Plan the story using your answers to questions 1 and 2, and include your verdict on whether Elizabeth seems to have been a success. Then write out your story.

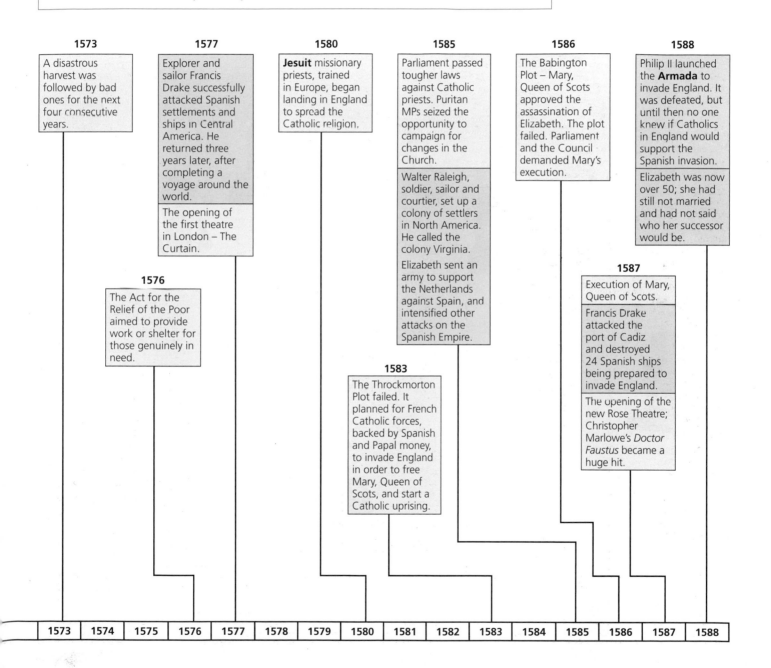

1573
A disastrous harvest was followed by bad ones for the next four consecutive years.

1577
Explorer and sailor Francis Drake successfully attacked Spanish settlements and ships in Central America. He returned three years later, after completing a voyage around the world.

The opening of the first theatre in London – The Curtain.

1576
The Act for the Relief of the Poor aimed to provide work or shelter for those genuinely in need.

1580
Jesuit missionary priests, trained in Europe, began landing in England to spread the Catholic religion.

1583
The Throckmorton Plot failed. It planned for French Catholic forces, backed by Spanish and Papal money, to invade England in order to free Mary, Queen of Scots, and start a Catholic uprising.

1585
Parliament passed tougher laws against Catholic priests. Puritan MPs seized the opportunity to campaign for changes in the Church.

Walter Raleigh, soldier, sailor and courtier, set up a colony of settlers in North America. He called the colony Virginia.

Elizabeth sent an army to support the Netherlands against Spain, and intensified other attacks on the Spanish Empire.

1586
The Babington Plot – Mary, Queen of Scots approved the assassination of Elizabeth. The plot failed. Parliament and the Council demanded Mary's execution.

1587
Execution of Mary, Queen of Scots.

Francis Drake attacked the port of Cadiz and destroyed 24 Spanish ships being prepared to invade England.

The opening of the new Rose Theatre; Christopher Marlowe's *Doctor Faustus* became a huge hit.

1588
Philip II launched the **Armada** to invade England. It was defeated, but until then no one knew if Catholics in England would support the Spanish invasion.

Elizabeth was now over 50; she had still not married and had not said who her successor would be.

| 1573 | 1574 | 1575 | 1576 | 1577 | 1578 | 1579 | 1580 | 1581 | 1582 | 1583 | 1584 | 1585 | 1586 | 1587 | 1588 |

1.3 Who's who and what did they do?

You will meet many people in this book and you need to know more than just their names. You need to know what they did and the impact they had on events during Elizabeth's reign. This information is essential for explaining why things happened in Elizabethan England.

You will not remember them all straightaway, but you can make a good start by completing the activity below and then keep working at remembering who's who. After a while, you will be surprised how well you know 'who's who'.

WHO WAS WHO IN ELIZABETH'S REIGN?

1. Draw your own copy of the diagram on these two pages. Find out what each person did and their religion, by looking them up in this book, and add a brief description to your chart.

2. If there is something special about a particular person or group's relationship with the Queen, write that along a line drawn between Elizabeth and the person or group.

3. Some of the people here are shown in silhouette form rather than portrait. Can you suggest why this is?

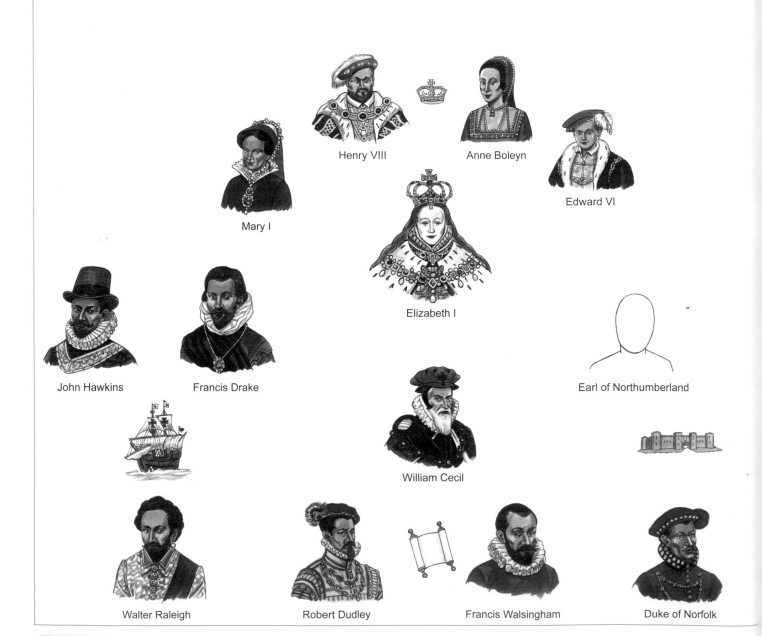

Henry VIII

Anne Boleyn

Edward VI

Mary I

Elizabeth I

John Hawkins

Francis Drake

William Cecil

Earl of Northumberland

Walter Raleigh

Robert Dudley

Francis Walsingham

Duke of Norfolk

You could do this activity physically in the classroom, using ribbons or string, with each of you 'playing' one of the characters and telling the others who you were, which other people you were connected to and what your role was in Elizabeth's reign. If you are brave enough, you could also explain what you thought of Elizabeth!

?

The Pope

Mary Queen of Scots

Philip II

Earl of Westmorland

Roberto Ridolfi

Francis Throckmorton

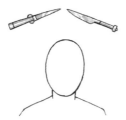

Anthony Babington

Confusion warnings!

Confusion over names is a common problem for students. Here are two examples:

A. There were two Queen Marys in the sixteenth century.

   1. Mary I of England, also called Mary Tudor. She was Elizabeth's half-sister and ruled England before her, from 1553 to 1558.
   2. Queen Mary of Scotland, also called Mary, Queen of Scots. She was Elizabeth's cousin. She ruled Scotland from 1560 to 1568. In 1568 she was imprisoned in England.

   Remember – Mary I had died before Elizabeth became Queen. It was Mary, Queen of Scots who was alive and dangerous throughout Elizabeth's reign.

Mary I	Elizabeth	Mary, Queen of Scots
Elizabeth's half-sister DIED 1558		Elizabeth's rival EXECUTED 1587

B. Some people are known by two different names! Robert Dudley was the Earl of Leicester, and some books call him Dudley, while others refer to him as Leicester. You need to know that this was the same man. In your diagram from the activity on page 6, make sure you include a person's title as well as their name.

1.4 Getting better at History – why are we making learning visible?

This book does not just tell you about Elizabeth and the events of her reign. It is also about what you have to do to get better at History and so get the best possible grade in your exam. One way we will help you is by identifying common mistakes that students make and so help you to avoid them.

We began on the last page by highlighting the importance of identifying all the key individuals and giving you tasks to get to know them. Confusing individuals is a common mistake students make. Another is to underestimate the importance of religion in the sixteenth century; page 9 helps you to understand this more clearly.

However, what happens when you meet new information and feel puzzled, maybe even totally confused? You have two choices:

> Muddle on, try to ignore or hide the problem and do not tell your teacher. You may lose confidence and stop working hard.
>
> The result – you make mistakes in your exams and do badly.

Choice A

> Think about why you are puzzled and **identify** the problem. Then admit there is something you do not understand and tell your teacher.
>
> The result – your teacher helps you to sort out the problem, your confidence increases and you do well in your exams.

Choice B

Choice B is a lot smarter than the Choice A! With Choice B, you are taking responsibility for your own learning and your own success. It may sound strange, but one crucial way to get better at History is to admit when you are confused and getting things wrong – then you can start to put things right.

We emphasised one very important word in Choice B – identify. You cannot get better at History unless you and your teacher identify exactly what you do not know and understand. To put that another way, you have to make that problem visible before you can put it right.

Visible learning

It is okay to get things wrong. We all do. And often, the things we get wrong and then correct are the things we remember best, because we have had to think harder about them. Saying, 'I do not understand,' is the first step towards getting it right.

WHAT ARE YOUR STRENGTHS IN HISTORY?

1. What are the main points in the section headed 'Getting better at History'?
2. Which aspects of History have you been good at in Key Stage 3 and other parts of your GCSE course (if you have already studied other topics)?
3. What are you not so good at in History and how could you improve?

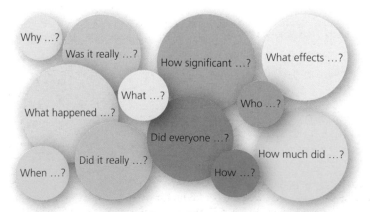

ASKING QUESTIONS ABOUT ELIZABETH

One of the skills we want you to develop is the ability to ask your own good History questions. What questions do you want to ask about Elizabeth, her reign and her reputation?

Use the question starters shown as prompts for your questions. Think back to what you learned about the sixteenth century in Key Stage 3 to suggest answers.

1.5 The importance of religion in Elizabethan England

This page helps you to avoid the mistake identified on page 8 – underestimating how important religion was to people at that time. The story of Margaret Ward demonstrates how strong people's religious beliefs were.

The story of Margaret Ward, the 'Pearl of Tyburn'

Margaret Ward was born in Cheshire in the north of England, where Catholic beliefs were especially strong. Little is known of her early life, but at some point she moved south to London, where she worked as a servant. When she discovered that a Catholic priest was locked up in the nearby prison, Margaret visited him several times and smuggled a rope to the priest, who then escaped. Margaret was arrested by Elizabeth's officers because she had been the priest's only visitor. For eight days she was kept hanging by chains and was frequently whipped, but she refused to say where the priest was hiding. When she was brought to trial, she confessed her part in the escape and rejoiced that she had been able to free the priest. Elizabeth's government offered Margaret a pardon if she would attend the Protestant Church of England, but she refused. Margaret Ward was hanged on 30 August 1588.

Although the Protestant and Catholic religions were both Christian, people in the sixteenth century believed they had important differences (see pages 10–11), and many people strongly identified themselves as Protestant or Catholic. This mattered because people believed that their religious faith and how they lived their life would decide where their souls went when they died – any who betrayed their beliefs would be judged by God and despatched to hell rather than heaven. They were reminded of this every time they went to church by wall paintings such as the one in the **Last Judgement** painting.

THE IMPORTANCE OF RELIGION ?

1. Why did Margaret go to the gallows? (Think of answers from her viewpoint and that of Elizabeth's government.)

2. Which events shown on pages 4–5 also demonstrate the importance of religious beliefs?

3. Why is it important not to underestimate the importance of religious beliefs in the 1500s?

Souls who are saved climbing the ladder to heaven.

Angel weighing souls to decide their fate.

Devils boiling murderers in perpetual punishment.

Souls of sinners failing to climb out of hell.

Sinners being punished by devils in hell.

▲ Medieval churches displayed paintings of the Last Judgement where people could see them throughout services. The message was clear – people who had led good lives went to heaven to be with Jesus for eternity, but the torments of hell awaited all sinners and people who did not follow the right religion. People in the sixteenth century believed that their souls would go to heaven and hell for all of eternity, depending on how they had behaved in this life.

Religious divisions in 1558

The story of Margaret Ward shows that people in the sixteenth century were prepared to die for their religious beliefs. This made it very difficult for the new Queen to decide which religion the Church of England was going to be. Whatever she chose, some people were going to be angry and might even fight to change it. This explains why religion is central to your understanding of the entire period.

Religious groups

England had been a Catholic country under the authority of the Pope for nearly 1,000 years. In 1533 Henry VIII replaced the Pope with himself as Head of the Church and then set up the Church of England. Although the Church remained Catholic this move encouraged English Protestants. In 1553 Elizabeth's half-sister, Queen Mary I, had restored the power of the Pope but an increasing number of people, including Elizabeth herself, were Protestant.

Protestants were still Christians, but they did not accept the authority of the Pope or some Catholic beliefs. There were also some extreme Protestants, known as Puritans, who wanted an even simpler Church. Each group believed that they were right and only their religion would enable them to go to heaven after death. The boxes on these two pages outline the main differences in their beliefs.

Four key issues about her Church that Elizabeth needed to decide

1. The Head of the Church and the bishops

The choices facing Elizabeth here were fairly straightforward. She could follow her father, Henry VIII, and her half-brother, Edward VI, by making herself Head of the Church of England, or she could follow her half-sister, Mary I, and keep the Pope as Head of the Church. Similarly, she could run the Church by keeping its Catholic organisation, with archbishops and bishops at the top, or she could abolish bishops altogether.

Catholics	Protestants	Puritans
Wanted to keep the Pope in Rome as Head of the Church, and have a structure with cardinals, archbishops and bishops to help the Pope govern the Church.	Wanted the King or Queen as Head of the Church, with archbishops and bishops to help the monarch.	Did not believe in a Head of Church or bishops, and wanted committees elected by churchgoers to make the rules.

2. Decoration and music

The appearance of the Church was almost as important to people as the type of service they listened to. Traditionally, Catholic churches were built to show the glory and majesty of God and were as elaborate and expensive as possible, filled with stained-glass windows, statues, pictures and murals, wood and marble carvings, all dominated by huge altars and organs. Many people, not only the rich, left money in their wills for church

▲ Catholics and Protestants disagreed about what their churches should look like. Catholics liked richly decorated interiors to glorify God (A), but many Protestants (B) felt uncomfortable with so many images. Puritans wanted a plainer church still (C), because fancy altars, stained-glass windows and statues were not based on the Bible and so not approved by God.

decorations. Protestants, however, had begun to see spending this amount of money as going against the teachings of Jesus. When Edward VI made the country Protestant, he ordered the removal of all Catholic decorations from churches, but many of these were simply hidden away and put back later, in Mary's reign.

3. The clergy

In 1558, at the end of Mary's reign, all the clergy were Catholic. If Elizabeth was going to change the religion to Protestant, she would either have to replace all the clergy with suitably qualified Protestants or convince them to change their religion. Either solution was full of problems. Equally difficult was the issue of allowing the clergy to marry. Under Edward's Protestant Reformation, the clergy had been able to get married and many had done so, only to find in Mary's reign that they had to choose between their wife and their job. The most controversial difference, however, came over what the clergy should wear.

▲ The Catholics preferred richly decorated robes called vestments (A); the Puritans, plain black gowns (B); and the Protestants, something in between (C).

WHAT DID THESE RELIGIOUS GROUPS BELIEVE?

Read pages 10 and 11, which show the differences in four crucial areas between Catholics, Protestants and Puritans. Then complete a simple diagram summarising in a few words what Catholics believed about each of the four topics. Then create two similar diagrams, one for Protestants and the other for Puritans.

4. The Bible and Church services

At the end of Mary's reign, church services were Catholic and in Latin, as they had been for hundreds of years before Henry VIII's rule. Henry had ordered a Bible in English (rather than Latin) to be placed in every church, but services did not change that much until Edward VI introduced two Protestant Books of Common Prayer, which laid out services in English. These were overturned by Mary. So Elizabeth had a choice to make. The choice of service mattered to most people because only the right one would guarantee that their immortal soul would go to heaven.

Catholics	Protestants	Puritans
Wanted the Bible in Latin, read only by priests, and church services with the Latin Mass. Catholics believed that a miracle took place during Mass, when the bread and wine given to the people were turned into the body and blood of Jesus through the powers of the priest.	Wanted the Bible in English, which everyone could read, and church services in English with Holy Communion. They believed the bread and wine in the Communion service remained bread and wine, but were also the body and blood of Jesus.	Wanted the Bible in English, which everyone could read, and church services in English with Communion. They believed the bread and wine remained the bread and wine during Communion, and that Jesus was spiritually, not physically, present.

THE CHURCH OF ENGLAND: ITS ROLE IN SOCIETY

These differences might seem minor, but religious beliefs were incredibly important to people in the sixteenth century. Most people went to church every Sunday, and all the important rituals of their lives and daily routines were linked to the Church, including baptisms, marriage, holy days and harvest festivals. The Church was the centre of community life and supported the people through hardship. It also gave them hope, not only during this life, but by teaching that leading a good life would ensure eternal salvation. Not surprisingly, people thought their own beliefs were the right ones and all others were wrong. Europe, too, was divided by religion, and the rulers of Catholic countries, particularly those who were considering marrying Elizabeth, were watching closely to see what sort of Church and religion Elizabeth would establish.

THE ROLES IN GOVERNMENT

?

Look at the diagram on page 13. Describe the roles in government of:

a) the monarch

b) the nobles

c) the gentry

d) Parliament.

1.6 Elizabethan England in 1558 – society and government

Society

Elizabeth ruled over a population of about 3 million. Society was very structured, or hierarchical, with God, then the monarch at the top, going down through the ranks, to the labourers and poor at the bottom. It was still based on a rural, agricultural society, where wealth was determined by owning land, but the new merchant class shows the influence that the growing towns, especially London, were starting to have. The chart below tells you about the different social classes in more detail. Everyone was expected to know their place in the social structure and to look up to and perform services for the class above, while taking some responsibility for the class below. Not surprisingly, the wealthiest individuals came from the top classes, while the poorest were at the bottom.

> ### Elizabeth's government
> The government of Elizabeth I's reign was not what we would mean today by 'the government'. Elizabeth's government usually refers to her councillors, chosen by her and not elected.

God

The Queen

Monarch Made all the decisions, but was advised by leading nobles. Led armies in war, but there was no full-time royal army, so relied on nobles and gentry to provide soldiers. Enforced the law and punished criminals, but needed the nobles and gentry to keep law and order in each community.

Nobles and lords
(great landowners)
About 50 families

Nobles The wealthiest landowners, numbering fewer than a hundred, with huge local influence. They expected to be the monarch's leading advisers, to deal with crime and social unrest locally and to be commanders in times of war. Nobles could resent being left out of these tasks by a monarch. This could have dangerous consequences.

Gentry The next layer down, made up of lesser nobles, knights and lawyers. Although less wealthy than the nobles, they still owned land. The monarch needed the gentry to keep government running locally and to act as judges and sheriffs.

The gentry
(lesser landowners)
About 10,000 families

Wealthy merchants
About 30,000 families

Wealthy merchants Some merchants, especially those living in towns with a thriving port, were able to build up considerable fortunes from the profits of trade. Most mayors were merchants.

Yeomen (farmers who owned their own land) and **Tenant farmers** (who rented land from a landowner)
About 100,000 families
They could make money from the sale of surplus farm produce. Many yeomen had servants. Those who owned the deeds to their land could vote in elections.

Craftspeople, labourers, servants, the poor
About 500,000 families
Labourers could easily become destitute and join the ranks of the poor as a result of bad harvests, trading slumps or illness. In the towns they worked in trades such as textiles and leather and in the countryside they were employed as agricultural workers, usually on a seasonal basis.

Government

The structure of Elizabethan society was also reflected in the way the country was governed. By 1558, there was quite a sophisticated framework for running the country and imposing law and order. The monarch was responsible for all the big decisions, but could only rule effectively with the support of the politically important classes: the nobility and the gentry. The hereditary nobles of England were men of great power and many had blood ties to the royal family. They had considerable influence in local and central government. There were plenty of examples from History of unpopular monarchs being overthrown by angry nobles, each with their own private army. The diagram below shows the system of government. In the sixteenth century, the same people could hold more than one office, and serve the Queen through membership of more than one of the institutions you can see here.

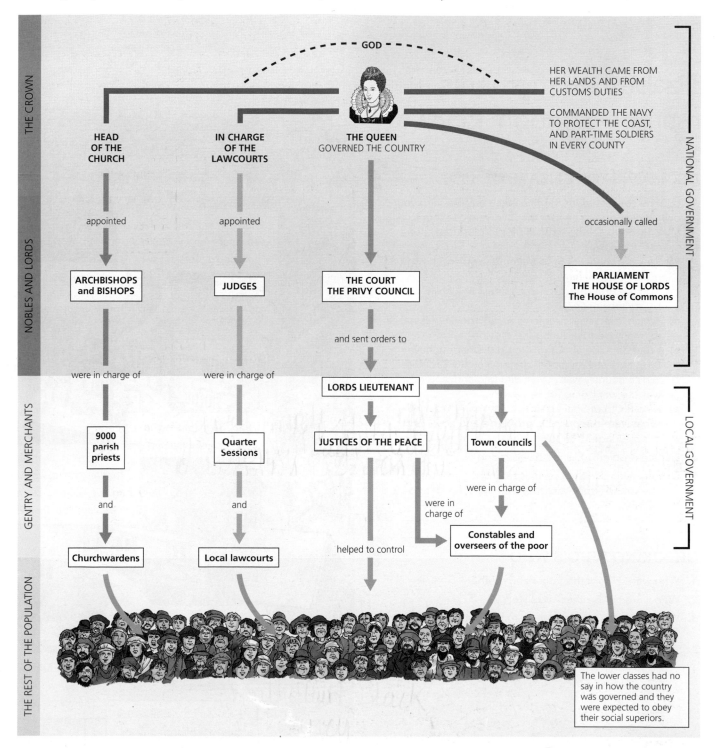

THE CROWN

NOBLES AND LORDS

GENTRY AND MERCHANTS

THE REST OF THE POPULATION

NATIONAL GOVERNMENT

LOCAL GOVERNMENT

GOD

HER WEALTH CAME FROM HER LANDS AND FROM CUSTOMS DUTIES

COMMANDED THE NAVY TO PROTECT THE COAST, AND PART-TIME SOLDIERS IN EVERY COUNTY

THE QUEEN
GOVERNED THE COUNTRY

HEAD OF THE CHURCH

IN CHARGE OF THE LAWCOURTS

appointed

appointed

occasionally called

ARCHBISHOPS and BISHOPS

JUDGES

THE COURT THE PRIVY COUNCIL

PARLIAMENT THE HOUSE OF LORDS The House of Commons

and sent orders to

were in charge of

were in charge of

LORDS LIEUTENANT

9000 parish priests

Quarter Sessions

JUSTICES OF THE PEACE

Town councils

and

and

were in charge of

were in charge of

Churchwardens

Local lawcourts

helped to control

Constables and overseers of the poor

The lower classes had no say in how the country was governed and they were expected to obey their social superiors.

Queen, government and religion, 1558–69

Elizabeth knew that as Queen she would face many problems. The imagined conversations on this page help you to identify those problems before you explore them in detail in Chapters 2 and 3.

Elizabethan moments in time – London 1558

DECISIONS FOR ELIZABETH, 1558 ?

1. Use the conversations in the speech bubbles and your own knowledge to answer the following questions:
   a) Why did it seem important for Elizabeth to marry quickly?
   b) Why did there seem to be more problems having a queen than a king?
   c) Why was Elizabeth's choice of husband likely to create tensions?
   d) Which 'everyday' problems had made life miserable for many people during the previous reign?
   e) What decision about religion did Elizabeth have to take, and why might her decision create problems?
   f) Which country was at war with England, and how well was the war going for England?
   g) King Philip of Spain proposed to marry Elizabeth. What were the possible problems and advantages of this marriage?

2. List the problems Elizabeth was facing in 1558.

3. Did any events in the previous reigns suggest that people would support Elizabeth? Look back to page 3 for information

CHECKING WHO'S WHO ?

1. Who were Elizabeth's father and mother?
2. Who were her brother and sister?
3. Who had been king or queen immediately before Elizabeth?

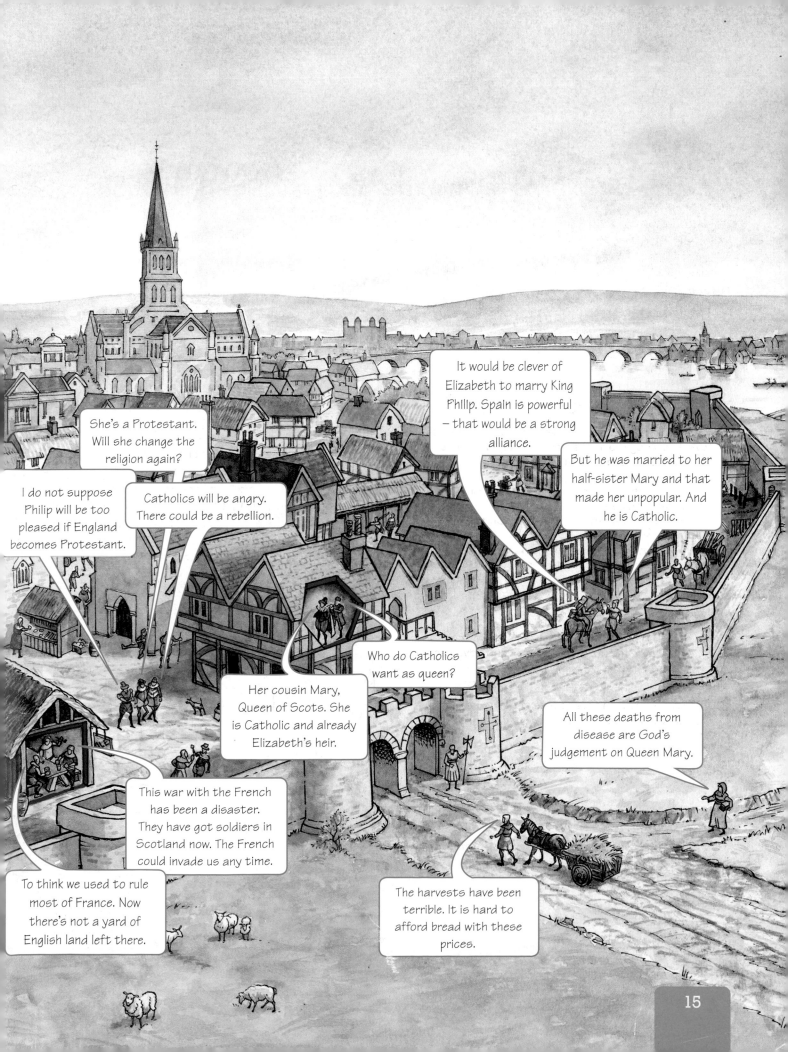

15

2.1 The problems facing the 'Virgin Queen' in 1558

In 1509, Elizabeth's father, Henry VIII, had been welcomed joyfully as a dynamic young king. Elizabeth's situation was very different. Many people were suspicious of having another queen after the disasters of her half-sister, Mary's, reign. Was it possible for a woman to rule England successfully or was a queen bound to fail? Later on in the reign, Elizabeth felt confident enough to use her gender to her advantage, encouraging the image of a powerful, independent 'Virgin Queen', who was married to her country, but in 1558, marriage was just one of many problems facing her. This chapter explores the problems Elizabeth had to deal with at the start of her reign and the choices she made.

ELIZABETH'S PROBLEMS ?

1. Look at the diagram below. What heading would you give to each problem?

2. Which two problems do you think were the most important to tackle straightaway? Explain your choices. Think about how problems might be dangerous to Elizabeth and what choices Elizabeth faced.

3. What advice would you give Elizabeth about how to handle the two problems you chose in question 2? Think about the events of the previous reigns (see pages 14–15).

Problem 1

Should she keep the Catholic religion or return to Protestantism? What penalties would be imposed on anyone who did not attend church? Elizabeth had to think about the possible reactions of people who did not agree with her decision. Would they rebel or even try to depose her?

Problem 2

All monarchs needed to enforce the law fairly and try to reduce hardship and poverty. If harvests, wars or other events went badly, then poverty, unemployment and high prices could increase the monarch's unpopularity and lead to rebellion.

Problem 7

Elizabeth's legitimacy or right to the throne was questioned by some Catholics, who believed that Elizabeth could not be queen because her parents' marriage had been illegal, and therefore Elizabeth was illegitimate.

Problem 3

Elizabeth had to take the important decisions herself, but she was expected to listen to the advice of the members of the Privy Council. First, she had to choose her councillors – would she choose just those who would support her, especially about religion?

Problem 6

Many people, including many of the wealthiest and most powerful nobles, thought a woman was too weak to rule the country. The issue of Elizabeth's gender and the expectation that she would marry were of national interest.

Problem 4

It was important to know who the next monarch would be if Elizabeth died young and had not married. People feared that if she died without a clear heir there could be a civil war, with ambitious nobles or foreign princes trying to seize power.

Problem 5

The two most powerful countries in Europe – France and Spain – were Catholic. England was at war with France, a war that had gone badly. France was allied with Scotland, which provided a base for an invasion of England. Defending the country was the monarch's most important duty, but a queen could not lead her army into battle. Defeat in war could result in Elizabeth being deposed.

Illegitimate The child of unmarried parents. The illegitimate child of a king or queen had no right to inherit the throne.

Elizabeth's character and strengths

Elizabeth was 25 years old when she became Queen. She had already had many experiences that prepared her for tackling the problems she faced. Her character was also very important in helping her deal with the problems and crises.

▲ This portrait shows Elizabeth at the age of 12 in 1545.

ELIZABETH'S BACKGROUND ?

1. Read the page below. Identify:
   a) two experiences when Elizabeth faced great stress and danger
   b) three personal qualities that would help her as Queen
   c) evidence that there were doubts that a woman could rule a country.

2. Look at the diagram on page 16. Which of the problems and issues in the diagram would the experiences and qualities identified in question 1 most help with?

3. Do you think that in 1558 Elizabeth:
   a) promised to be an excellent ruler?
   b) was potentially a good ruler, but that was uncertain?
   c) looked likely to be a failure?

   Explain your choice.

Her parents

Elizabeth's mother, Anne Boleyn, was beheaded for treason in 1536. Elizabeth was declared illegitimate and lost her right to the throne. When Henry's new wife (Jane Seymour) gave birth to a son, Edward, all chance of Elizabeth becoming queen seemed to have gone. Elizabeth now only saw her father and half-brother on special occasions. In 1543, when Henry married his sixth wife, Catherine Parr, she persuaded him to bring Elizabeth back to **court**.

Education

Elizabeth was brought up as a Protestant and learned Greek, Latin, French and Italian. She was taught Bible stories, dancing, riding, archery and needlework, and was especially fond of music. Roger Ascham, her tutor, wrote:

> My illustrious mistress shines like a star. So much solidity of understanding, such courtesy and dignity, which I have never observed at so early an age. She hath the most ardent love of the true religion and the best kind of literature. Her mind is free from female weakness and she is endued [blessed] with a masculine power for hard work. No memory is more retentive than hers.

Danger

In 1554, the new Queen, Mary I, suspected Elizabeth of being involved in Wyatt's Rebellion (page 3) and Elizabeth was accused of treason, which carried the death penalty. Eventually, Mary was advised that there was not enough evidence to put Elizabeth on trial. Elizabeth wrote to Mary that:

> I never practised, advised nor consented to anything that might be prejudicial to yourself in any way. Your Highness's most faithful subject, that hath been from the beginning and will be to my end.

Apprenticeship

Unless Mary had a child, Elizabeth was heir to the throne. Foreign **ambassadors** and English courtiers began to take far more notice of her. The Venetian ambassador wrote in 1554:

> her figure and face are very handsome, and such an air of majesty pervades all her actions that no one can fail to suppose she is queen.

In November 1558, Mary died and Elizabeth became Queen. The Spanish ambassador wrote to his king, Philip II:

> She seems to be greatly more feared than her sister and gives her orders and has her way as absolutely as her father had.

2.2 Visible learning: developing independence

On page 8 we introduced the idea of making learning VISIBLE – if you can see and describe how you go about learning, you will learn more effectively. Otherwise your brain just muddles along, without a route-map helping it to reach its destination. In History, that destination is understanding a topic and being able to provide good answers to questions on that topic.

This page is a crucial example of visible learning. What you see below is your route-map – how to get from knowing a LITTLE about a topic to knowing a LOT about it. It is important because in the future you will need the skills to study independently, perhaps at A level, at university or at work. The route-map or process below will help you to work independently and effectively. The box below shows the process in six stages. Then the diagram explains it more fully.

Questions ⟶ Hypothesis ⟶ Research ⟶ Answer ⟶ Communicate ⟶ Revise

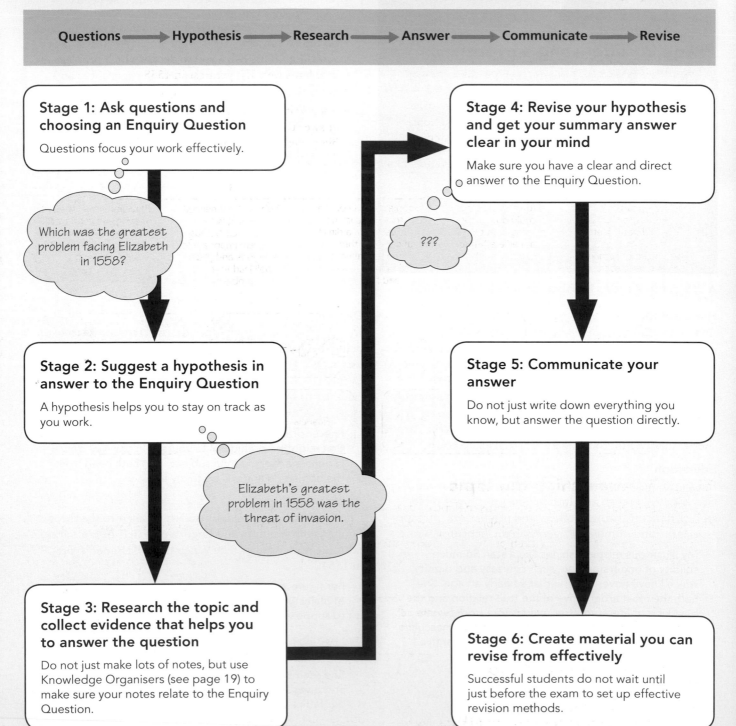

Stage 1: Ask questions and choosing an Enquiry Question

Questions focus your work effectively.

Which was the greatest problem facing Elizabeth in 1558?

Stage 2: Suggest a hypothesis in answer to the Enquiry Question

A hypothesis helps you to stay on track as you work.

Elizabeth's greatest problem in 1558 was the threat of invasion.

Stage 3: Research the topic and collect evidence that helps you to answer the question

Do not just make lots of notes, but use Knowledge Organisers (see page 19) to make sure your notes relate to the Enquiry Question.

Stage 4: Revise your hypothesis and get your summary answer clear in your mind

Make sure you have a clear and direct answer to the Enquiry Question.

???

Stage 5: Communicate your answer

Do not just write down everything you know, but answer the question directly.

Stage 6: Create material you can revise from effectively

Successful students do not wait until just before the exam to set up effective revision methods.

2.3 Your Enquiry: Which was the greatest problem facing Elizabeth in 1558?

Stage 1: choosing the enquiry question

It was essential for Elizabeth to make a successful start to show she was not a weak ruler. This meant prioritising the problems. She had to decide what needed to be done straightaway: in other words, she had to decide '**which was the greatest problem in 1558**'. Elizabeth's situation therefore creates the enquiry question for this chapter.

Stage 2: suggesting a hypothesis

A hypothesis is your first answer to a question. Having a hypothesis in your mind establishes a clear line of argument, though you may change your mind later on. It helps you to keep the question in mind throughout the enquiry and stops you getting lost in too much information.

We will begin by suggesting a hypothesis:

Elizabeth's greatest problem in 1558 was the threat of invasion.

The first thing for you to do is decide whether you agree that this is a good hypothesis or if you would prefer to start with a different one.

1. Draw a continuum line like the one below and then place the 'problem cards' on it where you think they should go. This helps you to decide which problem or problems were the greatest in 1558.

2. Look at the position of the cards on your completed line. Write a paragraph summing up what you think the answer to the question is. This paragraph is now your hypothesis to develop as you work through this enquiry.

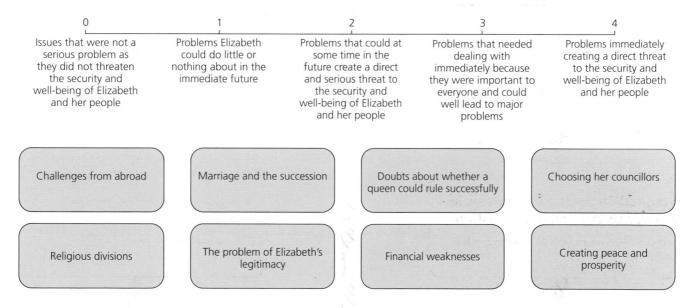

0	1	2	3	4
Issues that were not a serious problem as they did not threaten the security and well-being of Elizabeth and her people	Problems Elizabeth could do little or nothing about in the immediate future	Problems that could at some time in the future create a direct and serious threat to the security and well-being of Elizabeth and her people	Problems that needed dealing with immediately because they were important to everyone and could well lead to major problems	Problems immediately creating a direct threat to the security and well-being of Elizabeth and her people

Challenges from abroad

Marriage and the succession

Doubts about whether a queen could rule successfully

Choosing her councillors

Religious divisions

The problem of Elizabeth's legitimacy

Financial weaknesses

Creating peace and prosperity

Stage 3: researching the topic

Pages 20–28 explore Elizabeth's problems in depth. Your task is to collect evidence so that you can decide how great each problem was and which was the greatest problem.

3. Use a new piece of paper for each problem and draw a table on each one, as shown in the diagram below. After you have read about each problem, make notes under the headings in your table.

Challenges from abroad	
What was the problem in 1558?	
What were the choices facing Elizabeth?	
How great was the problem? (To answer this, use the criteria on the continuum line to guide you.)	

Visible learning

Knowledge Organisers

The continuum line and table are the first examples of Knowledge Organisers in this book. On page 8 we said we would help you avoid common mistakes, and one mistake is to make lots of notes so full of detail that you cannot see the main points you need. Knowledge Organisers focus on recording the key points you need. They will help a lot with revision later too.

2.4 Choosing her councillors

CHOOSING HER COUNCILLORS ?

1. Read these pages (20–21) and then answer the three questions in the table on page 19.

2. What does this statement by Elizabeth tell you about what she expected from her Privy Councillors?

   My meaning is to require of you nothing more but faithful hearts … for counsel and advice I shall accept you of my nobility, and such other of you the rest as in consultation I shall think meet [necessary] and shortly appoint … and they which I shall not appoint, let them not think the same for any disability in them, but for that I do consider that a multitude does rather make discord and confusion than good counsel.

3. If necessary, change the place of 'Choosing her councillors' on your continuum line and revise your hypothesis from page 19 after you have studied this topic.

In the sixteenth century, people believed that monarchs were chosen by God to rule the country. However, they needed the support and loyalty of the politically powerful classes. Each new monarch had to choose their own new councillors to help them rule.

The importance of the Privy Council

The **Privy Council** was the most important part of Elizabeth's government because it:

- contained men chosen as advisers and heads of government departments, such as the **Lord Treasurer**, who was responsible for the crown's finances and spending
- met frequently, sometimes daily, and advised on big decisions of state, such as war, religion and marriage
- was responsible for administration, such as overseeing finances, meeting foreign ambassadors, drafting correspondence and controlling the business of **Parliament**.

Elizabeth's choices

Choosing the Privy Councillors was a crucial task for Elizabeth. If she got it right, she would have a loyal team to help her run the country. If she got it wrong, she would have alienated some of the most powerful men in the country. The diagram below shows some of the issues she had to consider.

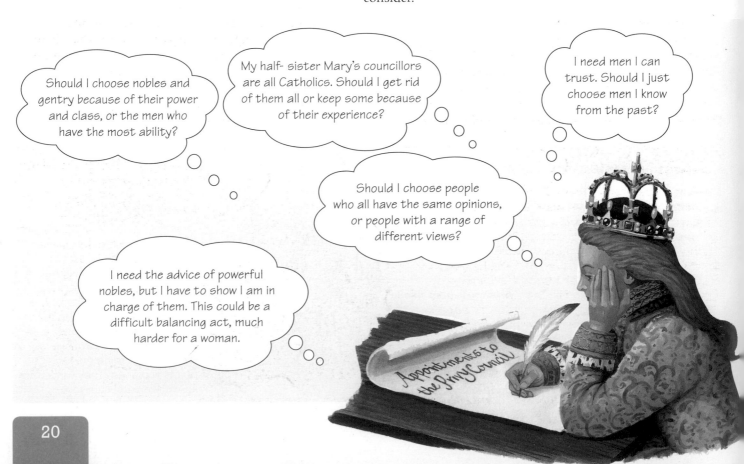

Should I choose nobles and gentry because of their power and class, or the men who have the most ability?

My half-sister Mary's councillors are all Catholics. Should I get rid of them all or keep some because of their experience?

I need men I can trust. Should I just choose men I know from the past?

Should I choose people who all have the same opinions, or people with a range of different views?

I need the advice of powerful nobles, but I have to show I am in charge of them. This could be a difficult balancing act, much harder for a woman.

Elizabeth's decisions

As soon as she became Queen, Elizabeth made William Cecil her **Secretary of State**, the monarch's principal adviser who supervised all government business, telling him:

> This judgement I have of you that you will not be corrupted by any manner of gift, and that you will be faithful to the state, and that without respect of my private will, you will give me that counsel that you think best …

Elizabeth appointed the rest of her Council quickly in the first three months of her reign, aiming for about 20 councillors rather than the 50 of Mary's reign. She was cautious and sensitive in her choices. She also thanked all the past councillors for their work, aiming to keep their support. Her caution is shown by the fact that she did not make her closest friend, Robert Dudley, Earl of Leicester, a councillor for another four years, realising the jealousies this might create.

Elizabeth was careful not to offend powerful men, and kept on the new Council about ten who had served under Mary, including high-ranking and powerful nobles with considerable experience and influence, some of whom had also served her father and brother. She chose her new councillors largely from her relatives and trusted colleagues, particularly supporters who had stood by her during Mary's Catholic rule. The full Council did not always meet. Much of the business of government was carried out by a small inner ring of Elizabeth's most trusted, inevitably Protestant, advisers, who worked closely with her.

Choosing the Council was the first issue Elizabeth had to handle. However she had had time to think about and plan who she would choose before she became Queen, in the months when Mary was ill. She acted cautiously and tactfully, but also decisively. She knew which people and what sort of Council she wanted, and she achieved this, apparently without any great upset. It could have turned into a problem, but it was to become one of the successes of her reign.

2.5 Financial weaknesses

The Privy Council, with the Queen, was responsible for every decision on financial expenditure, no matter how small, and was in constant touch with the **Exchequer**, which looked after the crown's money. In the sixteenth century, the monarch was expected to pay for all the costs of running the country, including the court and royal household, out of their own sources of revenue. These came from the rent or sale of crown lands, fines given by judges, **customs duties** on imports and **feudal dues**. If the crown needed extra money, usually to finance a war, it had to ask Parliament to approve taxation. Monarchs did not like calling meetings of Parliament to ask for money because it gave Parliament too much power.

In 1558, the royal finances had been severely strained by the war with France (see page 16) and Elizabeth inherited a debt of £300,000. In addition, most of the crown's wealth came from land ownership, and the monarchy had suffered from the same problems as other landowners in the sixteenth century. The rise in prices made it difficult for the crown, which could not easily increase its sources of revenue, mainly rents which were fixed, to keep up with this new expenditure (see page 19). Edward and Mary, however, had both introduced reforms to improve the running of the Exchequer and Elizabeth was able to build on these.

To strengthen the royal finances, Elizabeth severely cut back government spending right from the beginning of the reign, and strictly monitored the costs of her household. Exchequer officials were ordered to balance the accounts and make sure all debts were called in. Crown lands were sold off throughout the next twenty years, bringing £600,000 into the Exchequer. This approach took time to work, but by 1585, Elizabeth had not only paid off Mary's debt, but had built up a reserve of £300,000. The drain on finances and need for increased taxes approved by Parliament after that date was the result of war with Spain.

WILLIAM CECIL, 1520–98

William Cecil became an MP during Henry VIII's reign. His hard work and attention to detail earned him promotion to a principal secretary of the Council under Edward VI. As a moderate Protestant, he lost that post in Mary's reign, but instead worked with the then Princess Elizabeth. Like Elizabeth, he wanted to unite the country and avoid war, and tended to be cautious. As Elizabeth's Secretary of State, the most important position on the Council, Cecil made sure he knew everything that was going on. He controlled all government business, including the meetings of Parliament. He was not afraid to disagree with Elizabeth, but he was completely loyal and she trusted him totally. Between them, they ran the country for 40 years.

HOW GREAT WAS THE PROBLEM OF FINANCIAL WEAKNESSES

1. Complete your table from page 19.
2. If necessary, change the place of 'Financial weaknesses' on your continuum line and revise your hypothesis from page 19 now that you have studied this topic.

2.6 Challenges from abroad

Key

1 Mary I persuaded the Privy Council to commit English forces to the war her Spanish husband was fighting against France.

2 The French retaliated by strengthening their forces in Scotland along England's vulnerable northern border.

3 In January 1558, Calais, the last English fortress in France, was captured by France. This was a national humiliation, but Mary's government made no effort to win it back.

> Which countries were a threat to England in 1558, and why?

Scotland

When Elizabeth became Queen, Scotland was ruled by her cousin, Mary, Queen of Scots. However, Mary was living in France because she was married to the heir to the French throne. This strong link between France and Scotland, both Catholic countries, was a real threat to England. There were French soldiers stationed in Scotland, so England was in danger of a joint attack from across the Channel and her northern border.

France

In 1558, France was at war with both England and Spain. During Mary's reign, England had allied with Spain because Mary was married to the King of Spain. France also had a direct interest in the English crown. Mary, Queen of Scots, Elizabeth's cousin and heir, was married to the eldest son of the French king. France was a Catholic country and many Catholics thought Mary should be Queen of England. This gave France a motive for invading England on her behalf.

Spain

Spain was the most powerful and wealthy country in Europe. The Spanish Empire was made up of territories in Europe and conquests in Central and South America. Spain was a devoutly Catholic country, committed to preventing the spread of Protestantism. However, Spain and England had been friendly for most of the Tudor period, and King Philip II of Spain had married Queen Mary I, Elizabeth's half-sister.

The choices facing Elizabeth

The immediate problem facing Elizabeth was how to deal with the possibility of a French invasion. She had two options: to continue the war with France or to make peace. The table below shows you the arguments supporting each option.

Continue the war against France	Make peace with France
• A military victory would be popular and get the reign off to a good start. • Calais might be regained (page 3), which would restore English pride. • Victory would end the danger of invasion from France and Scotland. • Making peace might make Elizabeth look weak.	• England was only fighting because Mary had wanted to support her Spanish husband. Elizabeth and her councillors had no interest in continuing the war. • There was nothing to suggest that England could win. The Council did not believe England had the resources to recapture Calais. • England could not afford to continue sending aid to Philip II. In addition, the famine and epidemics of 1557 onwards had killed over 200,000 people. Farming communities were unable to spare men for fighting. • Defeat would get the reign off to a disastrous start and preoccupy a government which had other problems to deal with.

The decision

Elizabeth made her decision quickly. Peace was signed with France in January 1559, just three months after she became Queen, in the Treaty of Cateau-Cambrésis, and Calais was lost forever.

> **?** What does the speed with which Elizabeth made peace with France tell you?

How great was the problem?

Elizabeth spent over £100,000 at the start of her reign on military arms and munitions such as guns, pike-heads, bows and gunpowder. Restocking the realm's armouries required taking out massive loans, but is perhaps the clearest example that Elizabeth herself saw invasion as the greatest problem in 1558.

Despite the peace, fear of invasion continued. When Elizabeth decided that England would have a Protestant Church (see page 30), this increased the likelihood of a European **religious crusade** against England to restore Catholicism.

In fact, Philip II was more worried about the growing influence of France than Elizabeth's religion, so at first he kept on good terms, even though Elizabeth rejected his proposal of marriage. This did not stop the English believing that an attack from Catholic Europe was imminent and inevitable.

> **?** **HOW GREAT WAS THE PROBLEM OF CHALLENGES FROM ABROAD?**
>
> 1. Complete your table from page 19.
> 2. If necessary, change the place of 'Challenges from abroad' on your continuum line and revise your hypothesis from page 19 now that you have studied this topic.

2.7 Religious divisions

The diagram opposite shows the choices facing Elizabeth in deciding which religion everyone would follow in 1558. Monarchs, including Elizabeth, believed that everyone had to follow the same religion to make their country united. Differences in religion would lead to civil war and make a country too divided to fight back against a foreign invader.

1. Warnings from the past

Elizabeth had a great many issues to think about in deciding the country's religion. Firstly, she knew that religious changes in the past had led to protests and rebellions. The three paragraphs below shows you how strongly people felt about religious change, as does the story of Margaret Ward on page 9.

Henry VIII made himself Head of the English Church. Some Catholics did not believe that Henry could replace the authority of the Pope, including his friend, Sir Thomas More, whom Henry had executed. In 1536, when Henry closed down the monasteries, there was a major rebellion in the north, the Pilgrimage of Grace.

Under Edward VI, the Church of England became strongly Protestant. There were outbreaks of violence across the country. When Elizabeth's government introduced a new Prayer Book in 1549, Catholics in Devon and Cornwall rebelled.

Mary I married King Philip of Spain and restored the Catholic religion. This led to a rebellion led by Sir Thomas Wyatt. Many Protestants could not accept the Catholic Church. Mary burnt over 300 'martyrs' who refused to change their beliefs.

2. Warnings from abroad

Elizabeth also had to weigh the effects each choice would have on England's relations with other countries. France, Spain and Scotland were all Catholic in 1558. Foreign princes who were candidates for Elizabeth to marry would most likely be Catholic. In addition, the Pope, as Head of the Catholic Church, could excommunicate Elizabeth. If he excluded her from the Church, this meant he released her Catholic subjects from obeying her. He could also call on the Catholic powers in Europe to lead a religious crusade to overthrow Elizabeth and restore the Catholic faith under a Catholic monarch.

3. Divisions among the English people

Support for Catholicism

The majority of people in the country were traditional and did not like religious change. They were most likely to be Catholic, especially in the north, preferring decorated churches and priests' gowns, and services in Latin. To many people, the appearance of the Church (images, crosses, the priests' gowns, and so on) was as important as the Church doctrine.

As a result of Mary's reintroduction of Catholicism the clergy, the bishops, the Church doctrine and organisation were all Catholic. In weekly sermons for the last five years, the clergy had urged the people to resist Protestantism. It would be difficult to change all the clergy to Protestant.

Support for Protestantism

Elizabeth herself was a Protestant. In an age when religion and belief in eternal souls was so important, this was significant. Elizabeth appointed advisers who were mainly Protestant – they accepted positions on the Council in the belief that the new Church would be Protestant. Many devout English Protestants who had fled abroad during Mary's reign were also returning home, expecting Elizabeth to return to Protestantism.

In addition, the burning of Protestants in Mary's reign had made the foreign Pope and King of Spain really unpopular. A change in religion could signal a break with the past, allowing Elizabeth to be portrayed as the inspiration for a new English Church.

4. Elizabeth's dilemma

The difficulty of a compromise

It may seem that a compromise was the obvious and easy solution. However, a compromise ran the risk of pleasing no one. There was no toleration of other religions, so there would still be penalties for people who did not accept even a compromise Church. Elizabeth's options for a compromise were very limited. As a committed Protestant, she could not accept Catholic doctrine and beliefs, or the Pope as Head of the Church of England. Catholics could not accept a woman, even a queen, as Head of the Church. Puritans did not want a Church which had any signs of Catholicism. That left church decoration, music and the clergy where there might be some room for more flexibility. Finding a compromise would not be easy, but could mean a Church that was acceptable to the majority in England and less offensive to foreign powers. How many of these thoughts must have gone round Elizabeth's head while she tried to work out the solution to these religious divisions? The diagram below illustrates her dilemma.

5. Elizabeth's early moves

For the first few months, Elizabeth made few public pronouncements. She continued to worship privately following Protestant beliefs, but she kept some things linked to Catholicism – she had **crucifixes** and candles in her chapel, and liked the clergy to wear more ornate gowns.

Behind the scenes, Elizabeth and the Privy Council were drawing up a new Religious Settlement for the Church of England. Within just four months, they were ready to call a meeting of Parliament to pass the laws to establish the new religion.

> Elizabeth and her Council worked on the problem of religion immediately after she became Queen, and had a settlement ready to take to Parliament within four months. What does this suggest about the importance of the religious problem? **?**

I am a Protestant and so cannot restore the authority and teachings of the Pope.

Most people in England are Catholic, although my government is mainly Protestant.

The most powerful countries in Europe are Catholic.

Mary, Queen of Scots claims she is the rightful Queen of England and many Catholics support her.

Religious changes in the past have caused rebellions.

I want the country to be united and do not want to punish people just for their religious beliefs.

I need a national Church which most of my people can accept.

HOW GREAT WAS THE PROBLEM OF RELIGIOUS DIVISIONS? **?**

1. Complete the questions in your table from page 19 for this problem.
2. If necessary, change the place of 'Religious divisions' on your continuum line and revise your hypothesis from page 19.

2.8 Doubts about whether a queen could rule successfully

A woman should be a wife and she should be silent, obedient and domestic. A woman might rule her own kitchen but surely not her own kingdom; outside the kitchen she should be under the authority of a man, because she was physically, intellectually and emotionally inferior to men.

Women rulers in the sixteenth century were seen as both unnatural and a liability; they did not fit with the ideal of womanhood described above. Even the Queen's closest adviser, William Cecil, writing two years into the reign, told an ambassador off for discussing with Elizabeth, 'a matter of such weight, being too much for a woman's knowledge'.

Monarchs needed to keep their powerful nobles under control, to dispense justice and take harsh decisions, and to declare war and lead armies into battle. Women were seen as too weak to do this. The disastrous reign of Elizabeth's half-sister, Mary I, seemed to confirm these beliefs. She had dragged England into an unpopular war, in support of her equally unpopular husband.

There was nothing that Elizabeth could do to solve this problem in 1558, unless she married immediately and handed power over to her husband so that England had a male ruler; even her Council did not believe that Elizabeth would do this. Elizabeth could only solve the problem of her gender by proving that she was as good a ruler as any man and winning over her critics. This would take time.

2.9 The problem of Elizabeth's legitimacy

The problem of having a female ruler was made worse by the fact that some people did not believe that Elizabeth had a legitimate claim to the throne. Elizabeth's father, Henry VIII, had made himself Head of the English Church, and his Archbishop of Canterbury approved a divorce from his first wife. Henry then married Anne Boleyn. Elizabeth was their daughter. However, some Catholics believed that only the Pope could authorise the divorce of a monarch. Therefore, to them, Henry's marriage to Anne was not valid, Elizabeth was illegitimate and could not be Queen. The diagram below shows the logic of Catholic beliefs about Elizabeth.

Henry married Catherine → Henry replaced Pope → Henry divorced Catherine → Henry married Anne and Elizabeth born → Marriage not approved by Pope and so not legal → Therefore Elizabeth illegitimate

Realistically, there was very little Elizabeth could do about this. Even marriage and children would not change this view of her legitimacy. She could only go ahead, celebrate her coronation as the anointed Queen of England, and hope that in time she would win these people over. In her favour was the fact that she was the daughter of the much loved and admired Henry VIII, while Mary, Queen of Scots, was very closely linked to France, England's greatest enemy.

2.10 Marriage and the succession

People expected that Elizabeth would marry quickly and have children to provide the next Tudor monarch, the **succession**, and so ensure political stability. Marriage did not, however, mean that Elizabeth's husband would take over the running of the country in her place. When Mary I had married Philip II of Spain, Parliament had drawn up a marriage treaty which limited the power and influence he had in England.

There is no evidence that in 1558 Elizabeth had already made up her mind to remain single. Everything depended on the right candidate or suitor. In the early weeks of her reign, the court buzzed as foreign princes put forward their claims for the young queen's hand. Two potential husbands, Philip II and Prince Eric of Sweden, were politely turned down early on, as Elizabeth and her Council focused on the immediate problems of the war with France and religious settlement.

> **?** What does the speed with which Elizabeth tackled war with France and religion, compared with the priority she gave her marriage, tell you about how great a problem she thought her marriage was?

ROBERT DUDLEY, 1532–88

Elizabeth to Dudley, 1566: 'I will have but one mistress and no master.'

Robert Dudley was a younger son of the Duke of Northumberland and Elizabeth's closest friend. He was a leading English noble and a Protestant. In 1562, Elizabeth made him a Privy Councillor and, in 1564, he was created Earl of Leicester. They had such a close friendship that, by the 1560s, there were many rumours about their relationship, although he was already married. When his wife was found dead in suspicious circumstances, Elizabeth seems to have realised the impossibility of marrying Dudley, but their continuing closeness caused political and personal tension.

The real problem for Elizabeth was not whether to marry, but who she should marry. If she married an English nobleman, this might well cause anger and jealousy among other nobles. Marriage to a foreigner was at least as big a problem. Most of the princes of Europe were Catholic, and Elizabeth could not risk the hostility of her Protestant subjects. Her husband might also become the focal point for any Catholic discontent. All the time, Elizabeth had in front of her the example of Mary's marriage to Philip II, which had been so unpopular with the country. Perhaps if her Council and Parliament had united behind one candidate, she would have agreed, but they were usually divided. At some point during her reign, Elizabeth must have decided it was simply easier to remain single.

Later marriage possibilities

The question of marriage continued until the 1570s. As the Council and Parliament reminded the Queen for the next twenty years, it was her duty to provide an heir to ensure a peaceful succession of an English Protestant to the throne when she died. Archduke Charles (son of the **Holy Roman Emperor**, Ferdinand) remained a possibility for several years, but he was a Catholic and his proposal was opposed by Protestants on the Privy Council and in Parliament. Francis, Duke of Alençon (later Anjou) was the most serious of Elizabeth's foreign suitors. The courtship with the King of France's younger brother lasted most of the 1570s. The Council and the country were divided about whether Elizabeth should marry a Catholic and French prince and, in the end, Elizabeth herself, although she knew this was probably her last chance of motherhood, decided she could not risk it.

> **?** **HOW GREAT WERE THE PROBLEMS OF GENDER, LEGITIMACY AND MARRIAGE?**
>
> 1. Complete the questions in your table from page 19 for these three problems.
> 2. If necessary, change the places of 'Doubts about whether a queen could rule successfully', 'The problem of Elizabeth's legitimacy' and 'Marriage and the succession' on your continuum line and revise your hypothesis from page 19.

2.11 Creating peace and prosperity

Unlike today, rulers in the sixteenth century did not have economic policies. They wanted their countries to be prosperous because this meant their people would be more content and less rebellious, and also that they could ask for more money in taxes. They did not have much understanding of how and why countries became wealthy (or not).

Even more importantly, two of the key issues affecting people's prosperity – the quality of the harvests and epidemics of disease – could not be controlled by the monarch. However, poverty was still a dangerous problem for monarchs. Previous reigns had shown that, if there was a rebellion, people were more likely to join it if they were hungry.

Elizabeth and her Council were therefore anxious about food riots and other social unrest arising from poverty. Prices had been rising since the beginning of the sixteenth century. They rose very fast indeed in the 1550s. Many people found that their wages were losing value.

Nevertheless, people did expect bad harvests from time to time. Problems arose when harvests failed for consecutive years, as had happened, as you can see from the graph below, for much of the 1550s – leading to severe shortages of food. In Mary's reign, bad harvests occurred at the same time as flu epidemics, resulting in the deaths of about 200,000 people, either from starvation or illness, or presumably both.

Quality of harvest

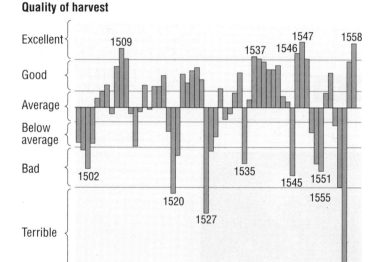

▲ Harvests, 1500–58

After several bad harvests in the 1550s, however, the harvest in 1558 was very good. This gave Elizabeth breathing space. Since bad weather was not under her control, she could only hope and presumably pray for good harvests; for the start of her reign at least, her prayers had been answered and there was no immediate problem.

HOW GREAT A PROBLEM WAS CREATING STABILITY AND PROSPERITY? ?

1. Complete the questions in your table from page 19.
2. If necessary, change the place of 'Creating peace and prosperity' on your continuum line and revisit your hypothesis in answer to the enquiry question after completing your table.

2.12 Communicating your answer

Now it is time to write your answer and ...

STOP! We have forgotten something very important. Look back to page 18 and the stages of your enquiry.

Revise your hypothesis and get your summary answer clear in your mind.

This is a really vital stage because one of the biggest mistakes that students make is starting to write their answer without having the answer clear in their minds. These activities help you to do that and they will work better if you do them with a partner.

1. Return to the continuum line on page 19. Use your completed notes to make your final decisions about where each problem goes on the line.
2. Use the completed line to write a paragraph summarising your answer to the question:

Which was the greatest problem facing Elizabeth in 1558?

Now it is time to write your full answer!

This chapter has given you a good deal of help, but you will find more guidance in the Writing Guide on pages 114–123. However, the person who will give you the best advice is your teacher, because he or she knows exactly what help you need to improve your work in History.

It's time to THINK about the answer

The Word Wall – language is power

Lots of classrooms have Word Walls for three reasons:

1. To help you understand the meaning of words and phrases that will help you understand Elizabethan England.
2. To help you communicate clearly and precisely, so you say exactly what you mean. This helps you do well in your exams.
3. To help you spell important words correctly. Marks are lost in exams for poor spelling.

You need to identify the words:

- whose meaning you are not sure of
- you cannot spell correctly every time.

Then make sure you find out their meaning and spelling. One way is to create your own Word Wall, on a piece of A3 paper, and add new words to it as you go through your course. Create a sense of achievement for yourself by showing them off and using them correctly!

Starting your Word Wall

The words below begin your Word Wall. Look back through Chapter 2 and start building up your Word Wall by adding more key words to it. The words in red are to help you understand the meaning of technical words and phrases that are used in this chapter, the words in green will help you communicate this information more effectively.

Practice questions

1. Describe two features of:
   a) the Privy Council
   b) Elizabeth's experiences before she became Queen
   c) Elizabeth's education.
2. Explain why religion was so important in sixteenth-century England.
3. 'The threat of invasion was Elizabeth's main problem when she became Queen in 1558.' How far do you agree? Explain your answer.
4. 'Elizabeth I dealt with the problems of 1558 successfully.' How far do you agree? Explain your answer.

Some of your exam questions (such as questions 5(b), 5(c)(i) and 5(c)(ii) in the exam paper) will suggest two topics you could use in your answer. You can see examples on page 114. We have not included topics in the practice questions in this book to give teachers the opportunity to change these from year to year.

Privy Council   succession   gentry

doctrine   clergy   illegitimate

potentially   uncertain

prioritise   immediately

This chapter has one overall enquiry, which we shall tackle through three mini enquiries, as you can see in this diagram.

Before we answer those questions, we need to find out about Elizabeth's Religious Settlement. What decisions did she make about the country's religion?

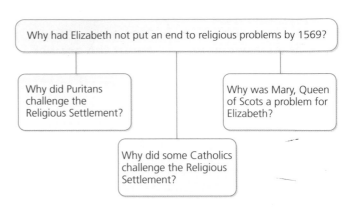

Why had Elizabeth not put an end to religious problems by 1569?

Why did Puritans challenge the Religious Settlement?

Why was Mary, Queen of Scots a problem for Elizabeth?

Why did some Catholics challenge the Religious Settlement?

3.1 Elizabeth's Religious Settlement, 1559

Elizabeth and her Council spent the autumn of 1558 drawing up plans for a new Church; then the Queen called a meeting of Parliament in February 1559. Elizabeth hoped her plans would be approved quickly, but there was some opposition, especially from Catholic lords and bishops in the House of Lords. Elizabeth responded by arresting two Catholic bishops, but she also reworded her plans, changing her title from Supreme Head to Supreme Governor. Parliament then passed the Acts of Supremacy and Uniformity, which established her government and doctrine of the new Church of England. England became a Protestant country again. The table opposite outlines the main aspects of the settlement.

Why did Elizabeth choose this settlement?

The Elizabethan Settlement of 1559 was a compromise, although it did reflect many of the personal religious beliefs of the Queen. Elizabeth had been brought up as a Protestant and disliked the authority of the Pope. She did, however, like decoration and ornaments in churches. She preferred priests to wear religious robes. Her Church looked Catholic, even if many of its ideas were Protestant.

For Elizabeth, the most important aim was to unite the country. She did not want religious differences to lead to rebellion. Nor did she want to have to punish people for their beliefs. Therefore, she chose a Church which she thought would be acceptable to the majority of her people. The result was that there were no immediate rebellions or major protests. Most people seem to have accepted the new Church.

ELIZABETH'S RELIGIOUS SETTLEMENT

Look at the table on page 31 and answer the following questions about the Religious Settlement.

1. Which aspects of the settlement had Elizabeth included to win the support of:
   a) Catholics?
   b) Puritans?
   c) moderate Protestants?

2. Which aspects of the settlement would each of the three groups dislike most?

3. Apart from passing laws, how else did Elizabeth try to win people over to the new Church?

4. How cleverly do you think Elizabeth had tackled the problem of religion at the start of her reign?

5. The main enquiry for this chapter is why Elizabeth still faced religious problems in 1569, ten years after she made this settlement. What reasons can you suggest now that you have seen the settlement?

What was the new Church of England like?

Area of concern	What Elizabeth had ordered in the Religious Settlement of 1559	Impact
Head of the Church and the Bishops	Elizabeth, not the Pope, was now Head of the Church, but the title she gave herself was Supreme Governor. All judges, government officials, MPs and clergy had to take an oath accepting Elizabeth's title. If they refused, they could be imprisoned. If they refused three times, they could be executed. Bishops would run the Church.	This was acceptable to all but a few. Ordinary Catholics accepted the title Governor, as they could tell themselves that the Pope was still the Head of the Church. All but one of Mary's Catholic bishops resigned rather than take the oath.
Church decoration and music	Ornaments and decoration were allowed in churches. The singing of hymns continued.	The appearance of the church was very important to the people. By making no changes, Elizabeth was winning many of them over, although the Puritan bishops always complained that the new Church looked too Catholic.
The Bible and church services	The Bible and church services had to be in English. Every church had to have a Bible written in English. A new Protestant Prayer Book had to be used in every church. Bread and wine were to be offered during Holy Communion, but the reasons why were left vague (see page 11).	The omission of Latin Mass was unacceptable to Catholics. Many got round this, however, by going to the new Church on Sundays and then taking Mass secretly later. Elizabeth's government knew this was going on, but did nothing as long as Catholics appeared to be loyal.
The clergy	All clergy had to take an oath, recognising Elizabeth's title and agreeing to use the new Prayer Book. The clergy had to wear a surplice, rather than the plain black gowns the Puritans preferred, but unlike Catholic priests, they were now allowed to marry. All preachers had to have a licence and had to preach at least once a month.	Most churchmen took the oath of loyalty to the new Church. Only 250 out of 9,000 priests refused and lost their jobs. This meant that most people would go their usual church on a Sunday and hear services conducted by the same member of the clergy as before.

Elizabeth worked to establish the Church in the people's affections and to link loyalty to her with loyalty to her Church. The Church's role in society remained central: Elizabeth's subjects still went to church every Sunday to save their mortal souls, and looked to the Church for moral guidance, help in times of hardship, some basic schooling for their children and lots of village feasts and holy days.

How Elizabeth won support for the new Church

Encouraged the manufacture of medallions and engravings. These images of the Queen were not expensive and became popular, even replacing those of the Virgin Mary.

Attracted support by describing herself as the saviour of Protestantism. Elizabeth used biblical sayings and portraits of herself to show that she was the restorer of the true religion, bringing an age of harmony and progress after the chaos of Mary's reign.

Added her Accession Day to the calendar of Church festivals, so that a day of feasting, drinking and having fun would be associated with the Queen.

Made attendance at church a test of loyalty to crown and country. Recusants (anyone who refused to go to church) had to pay a fine of 1 shilling a week. This was a large amount for the poor, but not the rich. However, Elizabeth turned a blind eye when the fines for recusancy were not collected.

Licensed the clergy and told them what to say in their sermons. Every Sunday when they went to church, the people would say prayers for the Queen's safety and give thanks for the blessings of her reign.

3.2 Why did Puritans challenge the Religious Settlement?

Look back to pages 10–11 for a summary of Puritan beliefs.

THE PURITAN CHALLENGE ?

Read these two pages.

1. Describe two features of Puritan religious beliefs.
2. Why did Puritans oppose the Religious Settlement?
3. What powerful support did Puritans have?
4. How would you describe the challenge from the Puritans?
   a) Minimal
   b) Limited
   c) Considerable
   d) Great.
5. Write a short paragraph explaining why the Puritans' attitudes meant that Elizabeth still faced religious problems in 1569.

Puritan attitudes to the Religious Settlement

The Puritans were pleased that the new Church was Protestant, but felt that it did not go far enough. They believed it was too much of a compromise with Catholics and wanted a more extreme form of Protestant service, along with churches that were plain and simple. The diagram below shows what they were opposed to and challenged in the new Church.

Bishops running the Church
Puritans wanted the Church to be run by committees elected by churchgoers rather than bishops.

The Queen as Supreme Governor
Puritans did not believe in a Head of the Church.

The Catholic appearance of the new Church
Puritans wanted very plain churches: whitewashed walls and no stained-glass windows, pictures or statues; plain tables instead of altars, and no music.

Religious robes like vestments
Puritans wanted the parish clergy to wear only plain black gowns.

Some of the wording of the new Prayer Book
Puritans believed that the presence of Jesus in the Communion Service was spiritual, not physical.

Their disappointment did not stop some Puritans from accepting posts as bishops in the new Church. They hoped that this would put them in a good position to move the Church in a Puritan direction. Some Puritans were very influential. Some were MPs in the House of Commons and some, like the Earl of Leicester and Sir Francis Walsingham, were members of the Queen's Council.

The Puritans did try to persuade Elizabeth to make changes. Between 1559 and 1563, bishops pushed for the removal of those things that they felt were 'too Catholic'. These included holy days, using the sign of the cross, organ music and, above all, they campaigned continually for the wearing of plain black gowns. Elizabeth refused to agree to the Puritans' wishes for more change. Some Puritan MPs who tried to make changes through Parliament in the 1570s were even imprisoned. The diagram shows her views about Puritans.

I like some of the old Catholic ways – there is nothing wrong with some decoration in churches and priests wearing vestments.

The Puritans are a minority. Most of my people like the Church of England. I must keep their support.

Some Puritans want to get rid of bishops. This would destroy my power to rule the Church.

The Puritans will never plot to overthrow me or help a foreign country to attack England.

I am in charge of the Church. Religion is one of my private matters of state. The Puritans have no right to ask for changes. They are attacking my authority.

PURITAN DIVISIONS

The Puritans were weakened by the fact that they were a small group, based largely in the south-east and London. They were not united, but were divided by their religious beliefs into:

- the Moderates, including the bishops, who wanted small changes, such as clergy wearing simple robes
- the Presbyterians, who wanted to get rid of bishops
- the Separatists, who wanted to get rid of a national Church completely.

Despite their differences, all Puritans agreed that it was better to have Elizabeth on the throne than the next in line, the Catholic, Mary, Queen of Scots. Therefore, they did not lead rebellions or violent protests, or try to help a foreign power invade England.

3.3 Why did some Catholics challenge the Religious Settlement?

The majority of people, certainly away from London and the south-east, were still Catholic. They remained strongly attached to their local parish church, with its familiar appearance and services. The hugely powerful noble families, especially in the north, were also still Catholic, as were many gentry. In addition, there were 8,000 clergy from Mary I's reign who had spent the last five years holding Catholic services. This suggests that there could have been mass opposition to Elizabeth's Religious Settlement, but this did not happen.

Catholic attitudes – acceptance

There was much about the settlement that was acceptable to most Catholics, as the table shows. Elizabeth had followed her own conscience in establishing a Protestant Church, but she had compromised because she needed the support of the Catholic political classes to help her run the country. As a result, even the great majority of priests took the Oath of Supremacy to Elizabeth.

▼ What most Catholics could accept about the new Elizabethan Church.

Leadership	• Elizabeth called herself Supreme Governor, not Head. • Henry VIII had made himself Head of the Catholic Church of England in 1533, so the English had had 25 years of getting used to their monarch running the Church.
Appearance and organisation	• Elizabeth's Church kept the bishops and archbishops, and all the clergy continued to wear ornate gowns. • Parish churches still had their stained-glass windows, organs and so on, so they looked and felt the same.
Enforcement	• Most penalties, in the Act of Uniformity, were in the form of fines for non-attendance. • Elizabeth did not seem to want to persecute people for their own beliefs, as long as they were loyal. • Elizabeth did not introduce punishments, such as the burning of Protestants during Mary's reign.
Nationalism	• After the disasters of Mary's reign, there was little enthusiasm for connections with Catholic Europe. • Elizabeth had created a uniquely English Church.
BUT	
There was no Catholic Mass as part of the services. For Catholics, this meant that their personal salvation – their chance of going to heaven – was at risk.	

Attitudes – opposition in England

In 1558, nobody knew how long the Religious Settlement would last. After all, the last two reigns had been very short. Therefore, people stored away Catholic images and relics and attended the new Church on Sundays. Some also went to Mass said by a priest at a local house.

However, some Catholics, known as recusants, refused to attend the new church services. They believed in the doctrine of the Catholic Church, especially the Latin Mass, and were not prepared to compromise. Many of this group regarded Elizabeth as an illegitimate heretic, the 'bastard daughter' of Anne Boleyn, and wanted her replaced by Mary, Queen of Scots. During these years, however, recusants worked quietly. Some of these priests became chaplains to the Catholic nobles and gentry, celebrating Mass in their houses, while others established secret meeting places where their former parishioners could hear Mass.

THE CATHOLIC CHALLENGE ?

1. Describe two features of Catholic religious beliefs. Look back to pages 10–11 for a summary of these.
2. Why did many Catholics accept the Religious Settlement?
3. Why did some Catholics challenge the Religious Settlement?
4. What powerful Catholic opposition was there in England?
5. How much help did opponents get from Catholics abroad?
6. How would you describe the challenge from Catholics?
   a) Minimal
   b) Limited
   c) Considerable
   d) Great.
7. Write a short paragraph explaining why Catholic attitudes meant that Elizabeth still faced religious problems in 1569.

Attitudes – opposition abroad

The attitude of the Papacy was vital for influencing the actions of European Catholic rulers, as well as Catholics in England. The Pope at the time of the Religious Settlement was Pius IV, and most people expected that he would excommunicate Elizabeth as an illegitimate, female, Protestant monarch. Pius, however, took no action, perhaps hoping that Elizabeth could be persuaded to change her mind. This gave the new Church time to establish itself, while leaving the Catholics in England without any support or leadership. When a new Pope did finally excommunicate the Queen in 1570, eleven years had passed and it was too late to be effective.

There was no support for rebellion from either France or Spain, two powerful Catholic nations. England was still an ally of Spain in 1559, even though Elizabeth had rejected Philip II's marriage proposal. In any case, Philip had no wish to lead a religious crusade against England, as he did not want to replace Elizabeth with Mary, Queen of Scots, who had strong ties with France – Spain's traditional enemy. In addition, he became increasingly occupied in dealing with Protestant rebels in the Spanish Netherlands and had neither the men nor money to spare. France, meanwhile, was involved in its own religious civil war from 1562, which would occupy it for the next 35 years.

Elizabeth's reactions to Catholic challenges

Elizabeth and her officials knew that Catholics were not attending church, but preferred to 'turn a blind eye'. Penalties were not strictly enforced because the Queen told her bishops that she did not want anyone to be vigorously examined over their religious beliefs. In addition, in the 1560s, she reintroduced some Catholic practices, for example:

1559 ornate gowns for clergy
1560 Requiem Mass for the souls of the dead
1560 candles and crucifixes remained in Elizabeth's private chapel.

At first, therefore, Elizabeth showed great leniency towards Catholics, as long as they were outwardly loyal to her and attended the new Church, which most did. Elizabeth was lucky that European powers gave no support to Catholics in England. She was able to deal with problems without any interference from foreign powers.

However, although Elizabeth was probably sincere when she said that she did not want to penalise people for their religious beliefs, she was unable to keep to this as fears of a Catholic invasion and plots against Elizabeth's life intensified: the arrival of Mary, Queen of Scots, rebellion in the North of England, and then the Jesuit missions. Acts passed by Parliament after 1571 identified 'active' Catholics who were hostile to Elizabeth and the Religious Settlement as political traitors and subject to the death penalty. An estimated 200 Catholics were executed in Elizabeth's reign, the majority Jesuit priests.

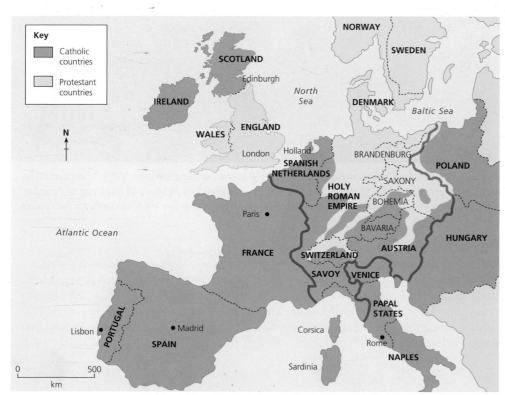

◄ How Europe was divided by religion in 1559.

3.4 Why was Mary, Queen of Scots a problem?

In May 1568, a fishing boat landed on the coast of north-west England, carrying an exhausted group of travellers. In their midst was a tall woman in her mid-twenties, wearing rough clothing, and with short, cropped hair. When she asked to speak to someone in authority, the group was taken to Carlisle Castle. Here, the young woman sent a message to Queen Elizabeth, asking if she would help her cousin by restoring her to her throne in Scotland.

The tall woman was Mary, Queen of Scots. She had been imprisoned by the Scottish government after she had married the suspected murderer of her second husband! However, she had persuaded her gaoler to let her escape and now she was in England, asking Elizabeth for help.

Mary's arrival created a major problem for Elizabeth. What should she do with Mary? Elizabeth decided to keep Mary in England as a prisoner, and Mary remained a prisoner for nearly twenty years. In all those years, Elizabeth refused to release or visit Mary, despite Mary's moving letters to her cousin.

▲ This portrait of Mary, Queen of Scots is thought to have been painted in 1578. The caption in the corner describes her as 36 years old, the Queen of Scotland, widow of the King of France and a prisoner in England. Mary had by this time been kept captive by Elizabeth for ten years.

> **?** Why would Elizabeth be anxious because Mary was Catholic?

Mary – Elizabeth's heir

As long as Elizabeth remained childless, her heir was Mary. Mary was Elizabeth's cousin and nearest relative, as the family tree on page 37 shows. Mary was also well aware of her position as heir. Since 1561, she had been displaying the English royal coat of arms to emphasise her claim to the English crown. This might not have been a problem, except for one very important issue – the cousins were divided by religion. Elizabeth was Protestant. Mary was Catholic.

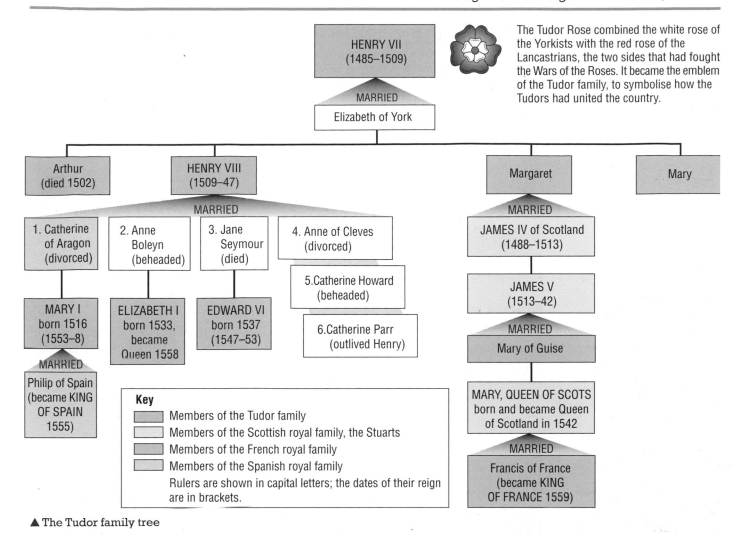

The Tudor Rose combined the white rose of the Yorkists with the red rose of the Lancastrians, the two sides that had fought the Wars of the Roses. It became the emblem of the Tudor family, to symbolise how the Tudors had united the country.

▲ The Tudor family tree

ELIZABETH'S OPTIONS

This activity explores why Elizabeth chose to imprison Mary. The table below shows the options Elizabeth had. Read pages 38–40 and then fill in the table with the advantages and disadvantages of each option. One example has been done for you.

Options facing Elizabeth	Advantages	Disadvantages
1. Keep Mary in England as a prisoner	Would keep Mary from causing trouble and perhaps leading a Catholic rebellion to take Elizabeth's throne.	Mary had not been proved guilty of any crime. As a prisoner, her relatives in France or Scotland, or other Catholic powers, might launch an attack to free Mary.
2. Provide an army to help Mary regain her throne		
3. Let Mary travel to France to stay with her relatives there		
4. Hand Mary over to the Scottish lords who wanted to put her on trial		
5. Allow Mary complete freedom of movement		
6. Execute Mary		

Mary, France and Scotland

Mary had strong links with France. When she was just a girl, she had been married to Francis, the son of the French king, and lived in France. In her absence from Scotland, the country was ruled by her French mother, Mary of Guise. Scotland was a Catholic country, but in 1559, Scottish Protestant nobles took control of the government from Mary of Guise. France threatened to invade Scotland, but then Elizabeth sent her own army to Scotland and the French backed down.

The result – Scotland was now a Protestant country, ruled by Protestant lords. Elizabeth hated rebels who had overthrown their ruler, because she believed that monarchs were chosen by God and should have the support of their people. However, she did not want France in control of Scotland, so gave support to the Protestant lords.

In 1561, Mary's husband and now King of France, Francis, died and she returned to Scotland, although she still had strong links to France. In Scotland she had to get used to a new situation – she was a Catholic monarch of a Protestant country where she had no power.

Mary's marriages

In 1565, Mary married Henry, Lord Darnley, who had a distant claim to the English throne through his grandmother. This marriage strengthened Mary's claim to the throne. So too did the birth of her son, James, the following year. This meant that anyone who wanted Mary to be Queen of England could argue that the line of succession was assured – they would not just be replacing one childless woman with another.

What happened next shocked the lords governing Scotland.

Henry Darnley turned out to be an unstable alcoholic, who treated Mary roughly while she was pregnant. Next, he ordered the murder of Mary's secretary, Rizzio, but soon afterwards, Darnley was murdered himself. In 1567, the house he was staying in blew up, but Darnley had been strangled first!

The chief suspect was the Earl of Bothwell – who then married Mary himself. This marriage shocked the Scottish government, who forced Mary to abdicate in favour of her infant son. Mary was imprisoned in Lochleven Castle, but as you have read on page 36, she charmed her gaoler into letting her escape and fled to England.

?

1. Why might Elizabeth be anxious about Mary's links to France?

2. Why would Elizabeth be reluctant to send Mary back for trial in Scotland?

3. Why would Elizabeth be reluctant to help Mary regain her throne from the Protestant lords?

Lochleven Castle, where Mary was held. ▶

Mary and Catholic opponents of Elizabeth

Mary was not just a danger to Elizabeth – she was a double danger. She was Elizabeth's cousin and heir, but she was also Catholic. To some Catholics at least, it was Mary who should be Queen of England, not Elizabeth. These Catholics believed that Elizabeth was illegitimate (see page 34).

As soon as Elizabeth declared that the new Church of England was to be Protestant in 1558, these Catholics had reason to oppose her, and to support Mary as an alternative to replace Elizabeth. If any foreign powers (such as the Pope, France or Spain) decided to launch a religious crusade against England, there might be Catholics in England ready to help make Mary queen.

Mary in England

This brings us back to Mary's arrival in England. Elizabeth had a difficult choice, and her problems are shown in the diagram below. Mary was not only her cousin, but also a queen. Elizabeth could not accept the idea that she should execute her cousin, who, as yet, had not been involved in any attempt to overthrow Elizabeth. None of the options was ideal. As is often the case, Elizabeth did not choose the best option when she decided to imprison Mary. She chose the 'least worst' option – the option that seemed to have the fewest dangers.

> 1. What were the dangers for Elizabeth if she gave Mary complete freedom?
> 2. Do you agree that keeping Mary in prison was the 'least worst' option?

Mary has a lot of support in Europe, especially in France, where she was married to their last king.

The Scots want me to send Mary back to Scotland to put her on trial, but I do not like helping subjects against their queen.

Mary is my cousin and appointed by God as Queen. It is my duty to help her.

As heir to the throne, Mary could attract the support of any discontented nobles who feel they have been excluded from power.

My Council wants to keep on friendly relations with the Protestant lords who are ruling Scotland, so that our northern border is secure.

Mary is far more dangerous to me here in England. Some English Catholics think she is the rightful Queen of England.

Some of my councillors and MPs think that Mary is too great a threat and want me to get rid of her.

▲ Mary in England – what could Elizabeth do?

Relations between Elizabeth I and Mary, Queen of Scots

The relationship between the two queens and cousins had its ups and downs over the years, although probably more downs than ups, as the boxes below show. It is difficult to know what Elizabeth really thought of Mary. Her letters to her were written in the flowery language of the sixteenth-century court, possibly with an eye on their possible publication at a future date! In reply to a request from Mary in 1568 that the two queens should meet so that Mary could prove her innocence in her husband's murder, Elizabeth wrote: 'O madam! There is no creature living who wishes to hear such a declaration more than I, or will more readily lend her ears to any answer that will acquit your honour'. Yet she never did meet with Mary, nor did she ever allow her to go free.

Ups:

1561: Mary returned to Scotland, but the country, thanks to support from Elizabeth, was now run by the Protestant Lords. Mary had little power and was initially friendly to Elizabeth.

1567: Elizabeth was shocked at the murder of Darnley and sent her sympathies to Mary, her 'sweet sister' and fellow monarch.

Downs:

1560: Mary started displaying England's coat of arms to show her claim to the throne. Elizabeth was furious.

1565: Mary married Darnley, who also had a claim to the English throne.

1566: The birth of Mary's son, James, strengthened the family claim and reminded Elizabeth of her own childless state.

1567: Elizabeth strongly criticised Mary for marrying the chief suspect in her husband's murder.

Further down still:

1568: The arrival of Mary in England, asking for Elizabeth's help in regaining her throne, placed their relationship at an all-time low and put Elizabeth in an impossible position.

1569: Elizabeth's preference was probably to restore Mary to her throne, through negotiations, not war, and subject to certain conditions, such as that Mary should give up attempts to secure the English throne.

Her failure to do this was due partly to her councillors, who did not want Mary back in Scotland, and partly to Mary herself. From the time of her arrival onward, Mary proved to be a schemer, writing to France, Spain, the Pope and English Catholics. Any possibility of Elizabeth securing her release by negotiation were ended by Mary's involvement in the plots and rebellion which you can read about in the next chapter.

▲ Henry Stuart, Lord Darnley. This painting is by an unknown artist and was painted in 1564, a year before his marriage to Mary.

THE PROBLEM OF MARY, QUEEN OF SCOTS

1. Why was Mary a danger to Elizabeth?
2. Look at your completed table from page 37. Why do you think Elizabeth chose to make Mary a prisoner?
3. How would you describe the challenge from Mary?
   a) Minimal
   b) Limited
   c) Considerable
   d) Great
4. Write a short paragraph explaining why Mary, Queen of Scots's arrival in England meant that Elizabeth still faced religious problems in 1569.

3.5 Communicating your answer

Now you have completed the three short enquiry questions for this chapter, you should have the knowledge and confidence to tackle any question about Elizabeth's Religious Settlement, like the one shown here:

Explain why Elizabeth had not ended religious problems by 1569.

The paragraphs you wrote at the end of each section of this chapter provide you with material for your answer. However, there is another, bigger reason you need to think about and include: a reason introduced in Chapter 1 on pages 14–15. This diagram helps you see the links between these reasons.

Puritans thought the Religious Settlement was too Catholic.	Some Catholics could not accept Protestant services.	The arrival of Mary, Queen of Scots in England gave Catholics an alternative to Elizabeth as monarch.

Religion was an extremely important part of people's lives. People believed that the way they worshipped God would help them reach heaven.

Writing your answer

Before you begin, think about:

1. How you will organise into paragraphs the reasons that explain why religious problems continued.
2. How great these problems were during the 1560s. Would you describe them as:
   a) very threatening
   b) occasionally threatening
   c) worrying
   d) not a threat at all
   or would you use another description?

You will find more guidance to help answer this type of 'Explain why ...' question in the Writing Guide on pages 118–119.

Practice questions

1. Describe two features of Elizabeth's Religious Settlement.
2. Explain why Mary, Queen of Scots created a problem for Elizabeth when she came to England in 1568.
3. 'Elizabeth's religious settlement was a successful compromise.' How far do you agree? Explain your answer.

Using your Word Wall

The selection of words below could be added to your Word Wall. Look back through this chapter and add other key words to it that will help you to answer this and other questions.

Supreme Governor   Acts of Supremacy and Uniformity

Communion Service   Latin Mass   recusant   abdicate

moderate   compromise   enforce   leniency   challenge

Queen, government and religion, 1558–69: review

We have reached the end of Elizabeth's first ten years as Queen of England. It is time to return to this book's big enquiry question:

Does Elizabeth deserve her successful reputation?

In Chapter 1, the popular view of Elizabeth and her reign, as 'gloriously successful', was introduced. After studying how Elizabeth tackled the problems facing her in the first ten years of the reign, you may or may not agree with this assessment. Some historians believe that what Elizabeth was really good at was creating a successful image and marketing herself. These pages explore how Elizabeth's reputation was created and why historians disagree about whether Elizabeth should really be seen as 'Good Queen Bess'.

The impact of film

You probably had images of Elizabeth in your head before you began this course, perhaps because you have seen some of the many films and television programmes made about Elizabeth.

?
1. What image of Elizabeth I does this film still create?
2. Do you think that watching films about Elizabeth will help or cause problems for you as a student?

◄ This scene is taken from the 1998 film *Elizabeth* starring Cate Blanchett. In 1558, at the time of her coronation, shown here, the 'real' Elizabeth would have been 25 years old. Compare this image with the portrait of Elizabeth on page 2.

Elizabeth's propaganda

One reason why it is difficult to be certain about whether Elizabeth was a great success is that she herself created propaganda to influence people's opinions. Like a modern celebrity, she made sure that everything that was made public about her was flattering. Few of her people actually met her, so portraits, especially on coins, were important propaganda. However, they rarely showed the Queen as she actually was. Professor Haigh suggested in his book, *Elizabeth I*, in 1988 that this propaganda may explain why some historians have been so positive about Elizabeth:

> The monarchy of Elizabeth was founded upon illusion. She ruled by propagandist images which captivated her courtiers and seduced her suitors – images which have misled historians for four centuries.

1. Why do you think her image was so important to Elizabeth? Refer back to pages 4–5 for ideas.
2. How did the 'Pelican' portrait create a positive image of Elizabeth?

◀ The 'Pelican' portrait was painted by Nicholas Hilliard in 1574, when Elizabeth was 41. Elizabeth's portraits were full of symbols that were understood by her people. Here, Elizabeth is wearing the brooch of a pelican on her bodice. The pelican, according to legend, pecked at its own breast so that its young could feed off its blood. This image therefore shows Elizabeth as the mother of her people, ready to sacrifice her life to protect them.

Later events and attitudes in historians' own times

In 1612, Sir John Hayward wrote:

> If ever any person had either the gift or style to win the hearts of the people it was this Queen. She was religious, magnanimous [generous], merciful and just. She was lovely and loving. She maintained justice at home and arms abroad, with great wisdom and authority. Excellent queen!

Hayward was a historian and lawyer who wrote in the reign of James I (1603–25), when there were many problems, such as the **Gunpowder Plot** in 1605. Such problems made men like Hayward look back at Elizabeth's reign as a Golden Age. This was not the only time when later events affected how people interpreted Elizabeth and her reign, as the first activity shows.

Historians' disagreements

Historians spend their working lives studying the sources that survive from the past. Their task is to describe the lives and events of the past and to explain why people did the things they did. This may sound simple, but it is actually very difficult, because the sources may disagree or may not answer all the questions historians ask. Historians therefore often interpret the past differently, as these brief extracts show.

Professor Christopher Haigh, writing in his book, *Elizabeth I*, in 1988:

> Elizabeth was not a wise and powerful statesperson, implementing the constructive policies she knew her nation needed: she was a nervous politician struggling for survival.

Professor Sir John Neale, writing in his book, *Queen Elizabeth I*, in 1934:

> It is difficult to convey a proper appreciation of this amazing Queen, so keenly intelligent, so effervescing, so intimate, so imperious and regal. She intoxicated court and country …

THE INFLUENCE OF LATER EVENTS ?

Sort these cards into matching pairs, linking each of cards 1–4 with one of cards A–D. Which event on A–D would have appealed to each historian?

> **1.** A historian writing in the late 1800s, during Queen Victoria's reign.

> **2.** A historian writing in the early 1940s, during the Second World War.

> **3.** A female historian writing in the 1970s.

> **4.** A Protestant historian writing in the seventeenth century, after laws restricted the rights of Catholics.

> **A.** Elizabethan sea dogs went on voyages of discovery to the New World.

> **B.** Elizabeth's navy won a famous victory against the Spanish Armada, saving England from invasion.

> **C.** Elizabeth set up the Protestant Church of England, despite attacks from Catholics during her reign.

> **D.** Elizabeth used her gender and status to her advantage to win the support of her people and show she was as good as any man.

ASSESSING ELIZABETH'S REPUTATION ?

1. How successfully did Elizabeth cope with the issues she faced between 1558 and 1569? Place the cards on the continuum line to decide whether her reputation should be a success or a failure for this period.

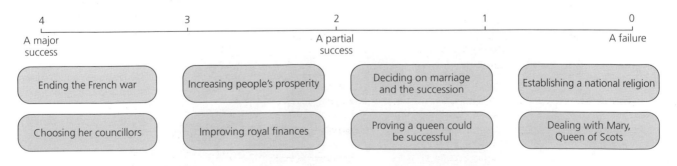

2. Do you think Haigh or Neale was nearer the truth about Elizabeth's first ten years as Queen?

Visible learning: revise and remember

Making your brain stickier

'I do not need to worry about revision. There will be plenty of time for that before the exams.' You might agree with the thought above, but before you turn over and ignore this revision page, take a look at the graphs below. They should convince you that leaving revision until just before your exam is not the way to success!

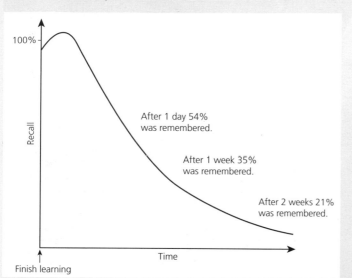

100%

Recall

After 1 day 54% was remembered.

After 1 week 35% was remembered.

After 2 weeks 21% was remembered.

Time

Finish learning

▲ Graph 1 The Ebbinghaus Curve of Forgetting. We forget the detail of what we study very quickly.

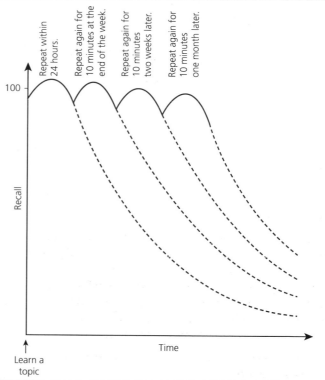

Repeat within 24 hours.

Repeat again for 10 minutes at the end of the week.

Repeat again for 10 minutes two weeks later.

Repeat again for 10 minutes one month later.

100

Recall

Time

Learn a topic

▲ Graph 2 How do you stop yourself forgetting?

1 Test yourself!

The more you think about what you have learned, **especially what you are not sure about**, the more chance you have of succeeding in your exam. So answer these questions – and they may come up again later.

1. Who did Elizabeth appoint as Secretary of State?	**2.** Who was England at war with in 1558?	**3.** How good was the first harvest of the reign?
4. What were vestments?	**5.** When did Mary, Queen of Scots arrive in England?	**6.** What was the name of Mary I's husband who proposed to Elizabeth?
7. List two reasons why Catholics disliked Elizabeth's Religious Settlement.	**8.** What language were the Bible and church services in during Elizabeth's reign?	**9.** List two reasons why Puritans disliked Elizabeth's Religious Settlement.
10. Which English nobleman did Elizabeth consider marrying until his wife died suddenly?	**11.** What did you find hardest to understand in this chapter? What will help you understand it?	**12.** Name one thing that you learned in this chapter that surprised you or that you now think differently about. Explain why.

2 Set questions yourself!

Work in a group of three. Each of you should set four revision questions on the first ten years of the reign. Use the style of questions on page 8. Then ask each other the questions – and make sure you know the answers!

3 Revise the big story

Keep the whole picture of the first ten years of Elizabeth's reign by telling the story as one of the following:

1. a historian
2. an individual who lived at the time. Choose from:
   a) William Cecil
   b) the King of Spain
   c) a Puritan
   d) a Catholic
   e) Queen Elizabeth.

Challenges to Elizabeth at home and abroad, 1569–88

This portrait was painted ▶ by an unknown artist in 1588 to celebrate the victory of the English navy over the Spanish Armada.

Elizabeth is shown as powerful and dynamic and much younger than her then 55 years. The painting is full of images showing Elizabeth's arrival on the world stage, alongside more familiar images from earlier portraits such as the pearls which symbolised purity.

?

1. What do you think the following represent in the 'Armada' portrait?
   - The window on the left
   - The window on the right
   - The globe
   - The crown
2. What is the overall image that this portrait is trying to convey?

(Answers can be found on page 125.)

The story of the Spanish Armada of 1588 is one of the most famous in English history. The defeat of the Armada is a major reason why Elizabeth is so famous and has such a successful reputation. The arrival and defeat of the Armada, however, was not an isolated event. It followed twenty years of rivalry with Spain and plots against Elizabeth's life – the events listed on page 47. It is also important to remember one thing from the beginning – when Elizabeth became Queen in 1558, Spain was England's ally, not her enemy. It was not inevitable that England and Spain would go to war against each other. Chapters 4 and 5 explore these events (pages 48–74), helping you to understand why Elizabeth often faced very difficult decisions, why she ordered the execution of her cousin, Mary, Queen of Scots, and why Spain became England's enemy.

?

CHALLENGES TO ELIZABETH, 1569–88

Read page 47 and use the information to answer these questions:

1. Which events outside England increased hostility between Spain and England?
2. Why did the following each increase anxiety about Elizabeth's safety?
   a) The excommunication of Elizabeth
   b) The arrival of Jesuit priests.
3. What evidence is there that Mary, Queen of Scots was a danger to Elizabeth?
4. In 1585, Elizabeth sent an English army to fight in the Netherlands. What do you think were the main arguments for and against sending this army?
5. Make a list of the possible reasons why King Philip of Spain sent the Armada.

The challenges facing Elizabeth at home and abroad

1568: San Juan de Ulua, Mexico

The third of John Hawkins's voyages to sell African slaves in the Spanish New World ended in disaster when the Spanish attacked the English fleet, killing all but eighteen men (see page 4).

The threat – ended hopes of expanding into lucrative markets overseas and increased tension with Spain.

1569: The Revolt of the Northern Earls

Catholic nobles in the north led a revolt to restore the Catholic religion, following the arrival of Mary, Queen of Scots in England and an unsuccessful plan to marry her to the Duke of Norfolk.

The threat – Elizabeth's government believed the rebels wanted to overthrow her as well as re-establish the Catholic religion.

1570: The Pope excommunicated Elizabeth

The Pope's excommunication of Elizabeth told Catholics they were no longer obliged to obey Elizabeth. This made it easier for them to consider plotting to overthrow her by force.

The threat – the Pope was calling upon Catholics, especially foreign rulers, to take action to restore Catholicism in England.

1572: The Revolt of the Netherlands

The Dutch rebelled against Spanish control. Philip II sent a huge Spanish force under the Duke of Alva.

The threat – the presence of a large Spanish army across the Channel was a threat to England's security. A great deal of woollen cloth was exported from England to the Netherlands. This important trade was disrupted, with harmful effects on the English economy.

1571: The Ridolfi Plot

A Catholic plot to replace Elizabeth with Mary, Queen of Scots, married to the Duke of Norfolk.

The threat – the plot involved the most senior English nobleman, the King of Spain and the Pope. It would have resulted in the overthrow of Elizabeth and the restoration of Catholicism.

1580s: Arrival of Jesuit priests from Douai, Belgium

Throughout the 1580s, English Catholic priests, trained at Jesuit colleges in Europe, returned to England secretly to save the Catholic religion.

The threat – the priests claimed their motives were only religious. However, their close allegiance to the Pope meant Elizabeth saw them as political traitors who wanted to replace her with a Catholic monarch.

1577–80: Francis Drake's round-the-world voyage

Drake attacked Spanish settlements on the west coast of South America, capturing large quantities of silk and Spanish coins, and seizing Spanish treasure ships.

The threat – a challenge to relations with Spain, but lucrative in terms of new trade routes and captured Spanish silver.

1585: War with Spain

Elizabeth sent an army to the Netherlands after the leader of the Dutch rebels, William of Orange, was assassinated. War with Spain was now inevitable.

The threat – England was at war with the most powerful country in Europe and fighting for its existence as a separate Protestant monarchy.

1583: The Throckmorton Plot

This plot planned an uprising of English Catholic nobles, supported by French forces and financed by Spain, to free Mary, Queen of Scots and restore Catholicism.

The threat – a combination of a religious crusade with widespread foreign support, resulting in the overthrow of the Queen.

1586: The Babington Plot

A Catholic plot to free Mary, Queen of Scots, which explicitly plotted the murder of Elizabeth.

The threat – it was obvious that as long as Mary, Queen of Scots was alive, then Elizabeth's life was in danger.

1587: The execution of Mary, Queen of Scots

Elizabeth finally agreed to the execution of her cousin and heir.

The threat – the Pope, France and Spain might invade England to avenge Mary. Her son, the King of Scotland, and English Catholics might also want justice and join attacks against Elizabeth.

1587–88: The Spanish Armada

In 1587, Drake attacked and destroyed 24 Spanish ships in Cadiz, but only delayed by twelve months the launch of the Armada, with the aim to land a Spanish army in Kent.

The threat – the Queen and government did not know how many English Catholics would join a Spanish invasion force.

4 Plots and revolts at home and abroad, 1569–88

Early on a grey February morning in 1587, Mary, Queen of Scots was escorted into the Great Hall at Fotheringhay Castle, where a crowd of about four hundred people was silently waiting for her. In the centre of the hall was a scaffold, draped in black. Mary, too, was dressed all in black, accompanied by two of her ladies-in-waiting. As she was prepared for her execution, glimpses of a scarlet petticoat could be seen beneath the black dress. Scarlet was the colour of Catholic **martyrs**. Mary was given time to pray and kiss her crucifix, and was then killed with two blows of the executioner's axe. Some accounts say that when her head was held up, a wig fell off, showing underneath very short, grey hair, and that, later, her little dog was found lying alongside the body, hidden in her dress. When Elizabeth learned the execution had been carried out, she was furious, and imprisoned her secretary who had sent the death warrant that Elizabeth had signed.

◄ The execution of Mary, Queen of Scots in the Great Hall of Fotheringhay Castle, Northamptonshire, 8 February 1587, drawn at the time by an unknown sixteenth-century artist.

4.1 Your enquiry: why was Mary, Queen of Scots executed in 1587?

As we explained on page 8, historical enquiries begin with questions. (The question for this chapter is the one in the heading above.) Then, you suggest a hypothesis in answer to the question, based on some introductory information. You could begin with a simple hypothesis, such as the following:

Mary was executed because she was a danger to Elizabeth.

However, if you think carefully about this hypothesis, using the information on page 47, you could change it or make it more detailed. These tasks will help you to develop your own hypothesis:

1. Draw a timeline for the period 1568–87, and mark the plots against Elizabeth, using the information on page 47. Include detail about who took part in each one.
2. Look at the pattern of the plots over time. Does the pattern support or challenge the hypothesis? Explain your answer.
3. Look back at the information on page 47. What other reasons can you find that might explain Mary's execution?
4. Rewrite the hypothesis above, creating your own first answer to the question.
5. To answer the big enquiry question, we need to find answers to a series of smaller questions too. Make a list of smaller questions that you want to ask to help you build a full answer to this question. Here is one smaller question as an example:
   Did foreign countries support the plots and so make them more dangerous?

Visible learning

Creating your own timelines

Creating a timeline for yourself will help you to remember the names and patterns of plots more effectively. This means you have to think, do the research and write down the details – this helps that information stick in your brain. It will not make the plots and revolts completely sticky, but we will give you more tasks to help with this later on!

4.2 The Revolt of the Northern Earls, 1569

Our big enquiry question is: 'Why was Mary, Queen of Scots executed in 1587?' To answer this, we need to find answers to a series of smaller questions:

- Were the plots a real threat to Elizabeth?
- Which plots were the most significant threat?
- Was Mary involved as leader of the plots?
- Were there other causes of her execution, besides the plots?

TWO NAMES, ONE REVOLT!

The Revolt of the Northern Earls is also known in some books as The Northern Rebellion.

On pages 49–56, you are going to study the Catholic plots against Elizabeth, beginning with the Revolt of the Northern Earls. The leaders, the Earls of Northumberland and Westmorland, were leading Catholic nobles. They strongly opposed Elizabeth's Religious Settlement (see page 35), but also had political and personal grievances. The information around the map tells you what happened.

THE REVOLT OF THE NORTHERN EARLS ?

What evidence can you find on this page of:

1. strengths of the revolt that worried Elizabeth and her advisers?
2. reasons why the revolt failed?

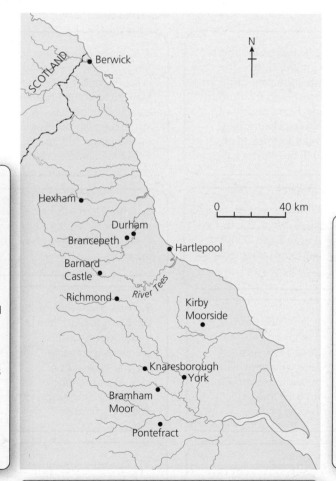

9–15 November: The Earls of Northumberland and Westmorland ordered all their tenants, the workers on their lands, to join their army and march south, to end Elizabeth's rule and restore the Catholic religion. Large numbers of men joined the Earls, putting their loyalty to their local lords before their loyalty to Queen Elizabeth. In Durham, the Earls and their men stormed into the Cathedral, pushed aside the startled Protestant clergy, destroyed Protestant prayer books and the English Bible, before overturning the communion table. Then they celebrated Catholic Mass in the traditional Latin.

However, there was bad news for the Earls. They had appealed to Catholic nobles in Lancashire and Cheshire for help, but these men stayed loyal to Elizabeth and refused to join the revolt.

22–30 November: The rebels marched south to Bramham Moor near York. The Queen had Mary, Queen of Scots moved south to a prison nearer Coventry, to prevent any possible rescue attempt. Elizabeth's government had also kept control of all the major northern towns, such as Berwick and York. When the Earls heard that the Earl of Sussex had assembled a huge royal army of 10,000 men in the Midlands, they turned back north. One rebel group captured the port of Hartlepool, hoping that Spanish troops would land there and support them, but no foreign support was ever sent to the rebels.

16–19 December: The royal army reached the River Tees and the rebels fled. The Earls escaped into Scotland, but Northumberland was handed over by the Scots and beheaded. Westmorland managed to escape abroad. Elizabeth ordered the execution of 700 rebels, although the number executed was probably nearer 450.

Why did the Revolt of the Northern Earls take place?

It is hard to find definitive evidence stating exactly what the two Earls (Northumberland and Westmorland) wanted to achieve. They issued proclamations, which said that their aims were to:

- restore the Catholic faith
- restore the political power of the northern nobility, both in the north and at court
- remove 'evil disposed councillors', who were influencing the Queen away from the true faith.

The Earls do not mention Mary, Queen of Scots or deposing Elizabeth. The Earls would have preferred a Catholic monarch, but it is uncertain whether they believed this could be achieved by removing Elizabeth's 'evil' councillors, by Elizabeth naming Mary as her successor, or only by murdering Elizabeth. Therefore we do not know which reason was most important to the Earls, but we do know the range of reasons which led to the revolt. The activity below helps you to understand those reasons.

THE CAUSES OF THE REVOLT OF THE NORTHERN EARLS

1. Which of the cards in this box provide evidence that religion was an important cause of the revolt?

2. Look at the other cards. Create a list of other reasons for the revolt. Some cards may tell you about the same reason.

3. Which actions by the rebels suggest that religion was the main cause of the revolt?

4. Which of these statements do you agree with? Explain your reasons.
   a) Religion was **definitely** the main cause of the revolt.
   b) Religion was **probably** the main cause of the revolt.
   c) Religion was **possibly** the main cause of the revolt.
   d) Religion was **definitely not** the main cause of the revolt.

> **1.** The Earls had political grievances against Elizabeth, as she had weakened their powers in the North. The Earl of Northumberland had lost an important position as Warden of the Middle March, defending the border against Scotland. Elizabeth extended central control from London by putting her cousin, Lord Hunsdon, in charge of Berwick, and she appointed the Earl of Sussex as President of the Council of the North.

> **2.** The rebels wanted to re-establish Catholicism as the country's religion.

> **3.** At the start of the revolt, the Earls stormed into Durham Cathedral and held a Catholic service.

> **7.** The Earls had already taken part in a plan to marry Mary, Queen of Scots to the Duke of Norfolk, the most powerful noble in England. They hoped this would help Mary to become Elizabeth's successor. However, nobles loyal to Elizabeth (such as the Earl of Leicester) had also been part of this plan, because they hoped this marriage would force Elizabeth to name a successor. These loyal nobles told Elizabeth about the plan.

> **8.** After Elizabeth found out about the Norfolk plan, she summoned the Earls to court. They feared prison or execution. They may have thought their only option was to revolt.

> **4.** Elizabeth had taken lands from these nobles, so their grievances were personal. Northumberland had lost copper mines, costing him money. Many northern nobles were facing financial hardship.

> **5.** The Earls wanted to get rid of 'evil councillors', such as Cecil, who they blamed for religious changes and their loss of political power.

> **9.** After the failure of the Norfolk plot, their more hot-headed followers wanted the Earls to take action. Lady Westmorland encouraged her husband not to back down.

> **10.** The Catholic rulers, Philip II of Spain and the Pope, appeared willing to support the revolt.

> **6.** The rebels wore Catholic badges and emblems.

> **11.** Government of the north of England was now carried out by the Council of the North, rather than by the traditional nobility.

> **12.** The Earls wanted Mary to be recognised as Elizabeth's successor and for her imprisonment to end.

How significant a threat was the Revolt of the Northern Earls?

You know what happened during this revolt and why it started. Now it is time to decide how much of a threat it was to Elizabeth. To decide, we need criteria – reasons why a revolt could be a significant threat to the monarch. The diagram below helps you to decide on a set of criteria – but you have to work out what they are for yourself!

WAS THE REVOLT OF THE NORTHERN EARLS A SIGNIFICANT THREAT TO ELIZABETH?

Each section of the spider diagram on this page provides information about a criterion that helps you decide whether the revolt was a significant threat.

1. What heading would you give each section? We have done one for you as a guide.

2. Where would you put each criterion on this 'threat line'?

```
0               1               2               3               4
```

| This revolt had no chance of success. | This revolt had some chance of success. | This revolt had a high chance of success. |

3. 'The Revolt of the Northern Earls was not a significant threat to Elizabeth.' How far do you agree? Explain your answer using your completed threat line.

4. Does the Revolt of the Northern Earls help to explain why Mary, Queen of Scots was executed? Think about this and jot down your ideas. We shall return to this on page 54.

Effective leadership

The Earls of Northumberland and Westmorland were not brave or decisive leaders.

The news that Sussex was moving towards them with a large royal army threw them into a panic, and they retreated and then fled.

Heading 2

The rebels never seemed to be sure whether to overthrow Elizabeth and replace her with Mary, Queen of Scots, or just to free Mary and have her named as Elizabeth's heir.

When Elizabeth moved Mary to a new prison, the Earls realised they could not rescue her anyway.

Heading 5

Elizabeth's government did not panic. Her officials in the north prevented the rebels from capturing important towns, such as York.

Elizabeth had no problem in raising a huge army to march north.

Several hundred people were executed for taking part – did this suggest that Elizabeth had been frightened?

Was the Revolt of the Northern Earls a significant threat to Elizabeth?

Heading 3

Most of the support came from tenants of the two Earls, who were expected to fight for their lords.

Appeals to the Catholic nobility to join the revolt failed completely.

Most English Catholics did not support the revolt.

Heading 4

Neither the French, the Spanish nor the Pope supported the revolt.

Although the Spanish ambassador gave the Earls the impression that Spain would support a revolt, King Philip II of Spain did not want Mary to be Queen of England because of her close links with France, Spain's enemy.

4.3 Were the Catholic plots really dangerous?

In question 4 on page 51, we asked you to think about this question:

Does the Revolt of the Northern Earls help to explain why Mary, Queen of Scots was executed?

The table below sums up the points you may have thought of:

How the Revolt of the Northern Earls helps to explain Mary's execution in 1587	How the Revolt of the Northern Earls does NOT help to explain Mary's execution in 1587
• It showed that as long as Mary was held in captivity in England, there were always going to be Catholics like the two Earls who would rebel against Elizabeth, in order to free Mary and restore Catholicism.	• The rebels did not come close to achieving their aims.
• Elizabeth must have been frightened to order the executions of so many people who were involved.	• It was another 18 years before Mary was executed, so it does not play a major part in explaining her execution.

The revolt does help us to understand that Mary was a threat and why Elizabeth and her councillors were worried, even frightened. It also helps to explain why her councillors tried so often to persuade her to execute Mary. However, it can only play a small part, at most, in explaining why Mary was executed in 1587, 18 years later.

> **REVIEW YOUR HYPOTHESIS**
>
> 1. Does the Revolt of the Northern Earls help to explain why Mary was executed in 1587? Explain your answer.
> 2. Amend your hypothesis from page 41 in answer to the big enquiry question, if you wish to improve it.

Continuing your enquiry

It is now time to look at the Ridolfi, Throckmorton and Babington plots. To assess the threat from each plot, you are going to use the five criteria from page 51 – you can see these in the table below.

1. Draw a chart like the one below. The example has been filled in for the Revolt of the Northern Earls.

	Were the leaders effective, powerful and dynamic?	Did they have a clear and realistic plan for overthrowing Elizabeth?	Was there a lot of support from the English people?	Was there strong foreign support?	Did the Queen make mistakes in dealing with the threat?
Yes – posed a significant threat					
Possibly – posed a slight threat			Revolt of the Northern Earls		
No – not threatening at all	Revolt of the Northern Earls	Revolt of the Northern Earls		Revolt of the Northern Earls	Revolt of the Northern Earls

2. Read pages 53–55 about the other three plots and make notes selecting evidence about the five criteria. Then fill in the chart.
3. Use your notes and completed charts to place each plot on the 'threat line' below.

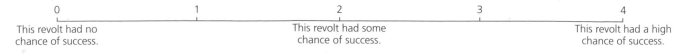

0	1	2	3	4
This revolt had no chance of success.		This revolt had some chance of success.		This revolt had a high chance of success.

1. The Ridolfi Plot, 1571

The plotters and their aims

Much is hazy about Roberto Ridolfi, other than the fact that he was an Italian banker, originally from Florence. Some historians even think he might have been a double agent, employed by Elizabeth's government to trap the Duke of Norfolk and bring about his execution. Mary, Queen of Scots used Ridolfi to carry messages to the Duke of Alva in the Netherlands, the Pope and Philip II of Spain, asking them to organise an invasion of England. Their aim was to overthrow Elizabeth, replace her with Mary, and then restore the Catholic religion. A coded document, outlining the invasion plan and listing likely prominent supporters in England, was left with the Duke of Norfolk. The diagram below summarises the aims of the plot.

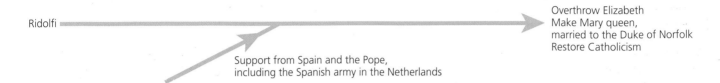

Ridolfi

Overthrow Elizabeth
Make Mary queen,
married to the Duke of Norfolk
Restore Catholicism

Support from Spain and the Pope,
including the Spanish army in the Netherlands

What happened?

In the spring of 1571, Ridolfi travelled to meet the Duke of Alva, the commander of the Spanish armies in the Netherlands. He explained to Alva how a Spanish army could successfully invade England and that this would cause the English Catholics to rebel. Alva does not seem to have shared his enthusiasm, because he wrote to his king, Philip II, suggesting that Spain should only invade after Elizabeth had been overthrown. Ridolfi, unaware, travelled on to the **Vatican** and then to Madrid. Meanwhile, in London, Elizabeth's government was carefully unravelling the details of the plot. Norfolk's servants betrayed him under interrogation and he was arrested in September. Ridolfi stayed in Paris, writing to Mary that he was going to 'retire into privacy'. After six months of letters and meetings, and thanks to the effectiveness of the government's information systems under Francis Walsingham, Elizabeth's Secretary of State, a plot which had never reached the public arena was over.

Consequences

The Duke of Norfolk was put on trial in January 1572, and was found guilty unanimously. He was beheaded on Tower Hill, London, in June. Ridolfi went to Rome, where he was made a papal senator, before returning to Florence, where he lived in considerable wealth until his death in 1612. Elizabeth expelled the Spanish ambassador, but relations with Spain did not decline at this stage. The plot did give Protestant MPs in Parliament the opportunity to put pressure on Elizabeth to be harsher to Catholics. The Queen agreed to execute the Duke of Norfolk, although not Mary, and to pass an Act saying that anyone who claimed she was not the rightful Queen was a traitor. Within weeks, news arrived from France that thousands of Protestants had been murdered in Paris, on the orders of Mary's relatives, in what became known as the St Bartholomew's Day Massacre of 1572. This increased fears of a Catholic attack in England.

THE RIDOLFI PLOT

Complete your 'significant threat' notes for this plot, and then fill in your chart from page 52. Then place this plot on the 'threat line' and make notes explaining your decision.

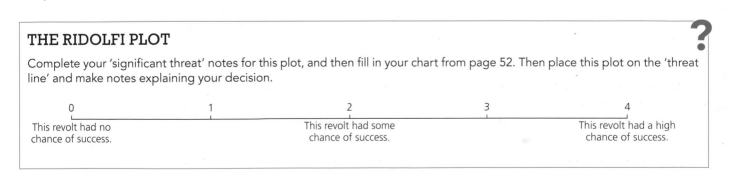

0	1	2	3	4
This revolt had no chance of success.		This revolt had some chance of success.		This revolt had a high chance of success.

2. The Throckmorton Plot, 1583

The plotters and their aims

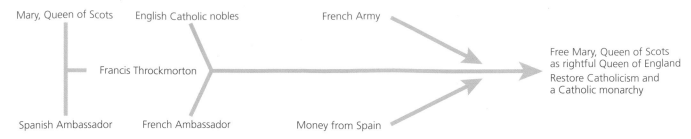

Very little is known about the man whom the 1583 plot is named after. The full details of the plot are also hard to uncover. Many key letters were destroyed by the plotters, and their aims were mainly confessed under torture. Francis Throckmorton was a young English Catholic, who came to the attention of Francis Walsingham and Elizabeth's government as the carrier of letters between Mary, Queen of Scots and the French and Spanish ambassadors. He was also in contact with members of the English Catholic nobility. Throckmorton confessed under torture that there was a plan for a popular uprising in the north of England, coinciding with an invasion led by the French Duke of Guise and financially supported by Philip II of Spain. The aim was to free Mary, Queen of Scots and restore Catholicism in England. The government, however, believed the target was the life of Elizabeth:

> The chief mark that is shot at is her majesty's person.

The diagram above summarises the aims of the plot.

What happened?

Throckmorton was put under surveillance at the end of April 1583, and in June, the government ordered his arrest. When his house was searched, papers were found that incriminated a number of leading Catholic nobles, as well as details of harbours suitable for an invasion force. Throckmorton claimed that the plan had got no further because the money promised by Philip II had not arrived. Evidence confirming the involvement of Mary, Queen of Scots is, perhaps not surprisingly, hazy. Throckmorton confessed that she knew of the plot, but later withdrew this, saying his statement was obtained under torture. Like the previous plot, this one was also discovered by Elizabeth's government before it could reach the public arena, so there was never any actual popular support.

Consequences

Elizabeth expelled the Spanish ambassador, Mendoza. Francis Throckmorton was executed at Tyburn in July 1584, and two nobles who had been implicated, Lord Henry Howard and Henry Percy, 8th Earl of Northumberland, were arrested. Henry Percy, brother of the leader of the 1569 Revolt of the Northern Earls, took his own life while imprisoned in the Tower. Henry Howard was released, after being questioned twice.

In July 1584, the assassination of William of Orange (see page 66) increased the government's fears that Catholics were seeking to assassinate Elizabeth too. The Queen herself wrote to the French ambassador:

> There are more than two hundred men of all ages who, at the instigation of the Jesuits, conspire to kill me.

They were worried that English Catholics, some of whom came from the ancient nobility, were just waiting for a signal from the Pope and military support from France or Spain in order to rebel against Elizabeth and depose her in favour of the Catholic, and in their eyes rightful queen, Mary, Queen of Scots. Elizabeth's government now intensified its efforts to protect her and Protestantism, against a background of approaching war with Catholic Spain. In particular, councillors focused on finding concrete evidence that would incriminate Mary, for they believed that Elizabeth would never be safe as long as Mary was alive.

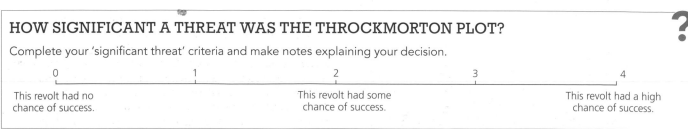

HOW SIGNIFICANT A THREAT WAS THE THROCKMORTON PLOT?

Complete your 'significant threat' criteria and make notes explaining your decision.

0	1	2	3	4
This revolt had no chance of success.		This revolt had some chance of success.		This revolt had a high chance of success.

3. The Babington Plot, 1586

The plotters and their aims

Anthony Babington was a 25-year-old Catholic, who had been a **page** to the Earl of Shrewsbury when the Earl was responsible for Mary's custody. He carried letters for her earlier in the 1580s, but in 1586, he seems to have been encouraged by his Catholic friends to join more serious plotting. Babington did not know that this latest plot originated from a fanatical priest whom Elizabeth's government had under surveillance. The plotters discussed, and put in writing, their intention to kill Elizabeth. The diagram below summarises the aims of the plot.

Men and methods employed by Walsingham to find evidence to convict Mary → Mary / Anthony Babington → Murder Elizabeth / Make Mary queen / Restore Catholicism

What happened?

In July 1586, Babington wrote to Mary, outlining six steps which needed to be taken to free the country from Protestantism. The first four involved planning for a successful invasion by a foreign army, probably Spain, with whom England was now at war; the fifth was the freeing of Mary; and the sixth was the 'dispatch of the **usurper**'. However, since the Throckmorton Plot, Elizabeth's government had been determined to find hard evidence against Mary. They had placed spies within Mary's household, who persuaded her it was safe to receive and send letters hidden in beer barrels. Mary could not resist. All the letters were intercepted and sent to Walsingham. When Mary replied to Babington on 17 July 1586 that the assassins would need 'four stout men furnished with good and speedy horses', her fate was sealed.

Consequences

Babington and two other conspirators were arrested as they attempted to flee. The rest were rounded up, tried and condemned to death for treason. They were executed in September 1586. In the same month, Mary, Queen of Scots was moved to Fotheringhay Castle, 120 kilometres from London, to begin her trial. The hearing of evidence and legal arguments lasted for weeks, but there was never any doubt about the conclusion. At the end of October, the **commissioners** found Mary guilty of plotting to take Elizabeth's life and recommended that she should be executed.

> **HOW SIGNIFICANT A THREAT WAS THE BABINGTON PLOT?**
>
> Complete your 'significant threat' notes for this plot, and then fill in your chart from page 52. Then place this plot on the 'threat line' and make notes explaining your decision.

> **DEVELOPING YOUR HYPOTHESIS**
>
> We began with a simple answer to the question, 'Why was Mary, Queen of Scots executed in 1587?' It was: 'Mary was executed because she was a danger to Elizabeth.' Since then, you have probably developed this to include more reasons or details.
>
> Now revise your hypothesis, writing a full paragraph, of six to eight lines, using the completed chart and threat line from page 52 to help you.

◀ Francis Walsingham was one of Elizabeth's Secretaries of State, and was responsible for protecting the Queen and the Protestant Church (see page 56). Walsingham's greatest success was trapping Mary, Queen of Scots into incriminating herself through the Babington Plot. He was also instrumental in persuading the House of Commons to pass stricter laws to protect Elizabeth against the Catholics. This portrait was painted by John de Critz the Elder in the late 1580s.

4.4 Catching the plotters – the work of Sir Francis Walsingham

Your work on the plots introduced Sir Francis Walsingham, Elizabeth's Secretary of State from 1573, but more often known as the 'spymaster'. Walsingham gathered together men who were skilled in intelligence and based them at his London home. The diagram below sets out the methods they used to identify and catch plotters.

The details below suggest this system was completely ruthless. For Walsingham, however, he was simply carrying out the policy approved by Elizabeth's government. From the Revolt of the Northern Earls onwards, the House of Commons kept up continual pressure on Elizabeth to execute Mary, Queen of Scots, and to increase the penalties against Catholics. Parliament succeeded in securing the execution of the Duke of Norfolk in 1571, and in passing acts in 1571, 1581 and 1585, which gradually increased the penalties against Catholics. Both Parliament and Council, many of whom were MPs, believed that the Queen, Protestantism and, ultimately, the realm, would never be safe while Mary was alive, and for twenty years they made sure that Elizabeth was aware of their views. However,

Elizabeth herself was not as ruthless as Walsingham, and she could overturn his plans. She changed the wording of Acts of Parliament so that ordinary Catholics did not suffer the same penalties as priests. She often delayed taking action against plotters (even when there was evidence of their guilt) because she thought Walsingham was too extreme because of his Puritan beliefs. Above all, Elizabeth consistently refused to execute Mary, Queen of Scots.

WALSINGHAM'S SPY SYSTEM ?

1. Describe two features of Walsingham's methods of catching Catholic plotters.
2. What do these methods tell you about how fearful Elizabeth's government was about plots against her?
3. Why did the Council and Parliament put pressure on Elizabeth, and how far did they achieve their aims?
4. Why do you think Elizabeth was moderate in her attitude to ordinary Catholics?
5. Do these methods help us to understand why Mary was executed in 1587? Explain your answer.

Intercepting coded letters and messages

The plotters developed increasingly sophisticated ways of communicating; some of Mary's letters were smuggled out in the heels of her ladies' shoes. Elizabeth's government kept on top on this, often by placing informers in suspects' households. Walsingham employed a man skilled at re-sealing letters so the plotters did not know they had been intercepted, and a leading code breaker who deciphered Mary's letters.

Searches and registers

Town councils were authorised to search foreigners' houses. The owners of taverns and inns had to report any foreigners staying with them. Customs officials also stopped and questioned travellers from overseas and could search them for papers, including messages and letters.

Using informers in England

The Lord Lieutenants of each county and the bishops officially reported any threats to Walsingham and everyone was encouraged to report suspicions of dangers to the Queen.

Francis Walsingham started his long career in government as an MP, and then worked for Sir William Cecil from 1568. He took over Cecil's framework of agents and reorganised it into an effective spy network. Walsingham was a ruthless and driven man, a workaholic in today's terms, who ran his spy network on top of his business as Secretary of State.

Employing a network of spies and agents

Agents with codenames were based overseas in major towns and cities, including France, Italy and Spain. Some were double agents, taking parts in plots against Elizabeth and sending information to Walsingham. Spies were deployed to root out information as events arose.

Interrogation and torture

Captured priests, such as Edmund Campion, and plotters like Francis Throckmorton, were tortured on the rack to extract information about their intentions and other threats to Elizabeth. Then they were executed as a warning.

Acts of Parliament

Walsingham was influential in Parliament, which passed Acts throughout the 1570s and 1580s, increasing penalties against Catholics, including the execution of priests. The 1584 Bond of Association pledged that in the event of Elizabeth's life being threatened, Mary, Queen of Scots was to be executed.

Capturing Catholic priests and recusants

After the Pope excommunicated Elizabeth in 1570, her government believed Elizabeth's life was in danger from Catholic fanatics. From 1574, the Pope started sending missionary priests to England. Walsingham's spies were particularly effective at seizing priests on the streets of London, with one Jesuit complaining: 'the spies so many and diligent as every hour almost we heard of some (priests) taken'.

4.5 Footsteps to the execution of Mary, Queen of Scots

THE ROAD TO EXECUTION

This is a good time to recap and sum up the sequence of events that led to Mary's execution.

1. The captions by the first three footsteps have been left unfinished. How would you complete them?
2. How great a part did Walsingham play in bringing about Mary's execution?
3. What evidence is there that Elizabeth was still reluctant to order her cousin's execution in 1587?
4. Which do you think was the most important step towards Mary's execution?

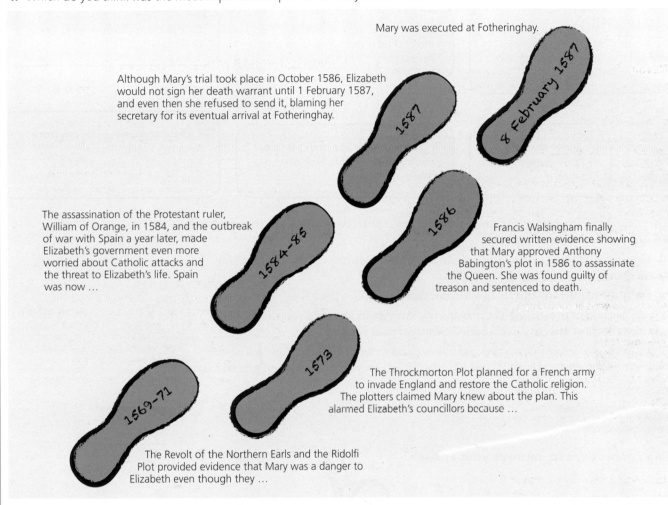

Mary was executed at Fotheringhay.

Although Mary's trial took place in October 1586, Elizabeth would not sign her death warrant until 1 February 1587, and even then she refused to send it, blaming her secretary for its eventual arrival at Fotheringhay.

The assassination of the Protestant ruler, William of Orange, in 1584, and the outbreak of war with Spain a year later, made Elizabeth's government even more worried about Catholic attacks and the threat to Elizabeth's life. Spain was now …

Francis Walsingham finally secured written evidence showing that Mary approved Anthony Babington's plot in 1586 to assassinate the Queen. She was found guilty of treason and sentenced to death.

The Throckmorton Plot planned for a French army to invade England and restore the Catholic religion. The plotters claimed Mary knew about the plan. This alarmed Elizabeth's councillors because …

The Revolt of the Northern Earls and the Ridolfi Plot provided evidence that Mary was a danger to Elizabeth even though they …

The puzzles of the death warrant

Although Mary had been found guilty of treason, she could not be executed until Elizabeth signed her death warrant. For two months, Elizabeth drove her councillors and Parliament to distraction by finding reasons to avoid doing this, despite their continual protests. Many historians believe she found it difficult to authorise the killing of a fellow monarch who had been divinely appointed by God, and that she was genuinely concerned about how other monarchs would react, not least Mary's son, who was now King of Scotland. Frustration and worry at these delays even made Walsingham ill. Elizabeth's Privy Councillors almost had to beg her to sign it, which she finally agreed to do at the beginning of February 1587. Even then, Elizabeth refused to send the warrant. On 3 February, a secret meeting of the Privy Council proposed sending it without telling Elizabeth, and began to make arrangements for the execution, which went ahead on 8 February. When she heard the news, Elizabeth was furious. She refused to speak to William Cecil for a month and imprisoned William Davison, who had taken the warrant, in the Tower of London for 18 months. On the other hand, she could tell James VI that she had never wanted his mother's execution.

4.6 Improving your explanation

By now, you have a strong understanding of the story of the plots against Elizabeth and how Mary, Queen of Scots was involved in them. This page provides activities to help you improve your explanation of Mary's execution, and so make your answer to the enquiry stronger and more effective.

1. The cards below show six major reasons why Mary was executed. Take each of the cards in turn, and choose two or three examples or pieces of evidence which prove that each reason played a part in explaining Mary's execution.

> A. She was Catholic and attracted the support of some Catholics who were opposed to Elizabeth's Religious Settlement.

> B. She was Elizabeth's cousin and so had a strong claim to the throne.

> C. The plots increased the sense of danger to Elizabeth.

> D. There was evidence that Mary knew about, and was involved in, plots against Elizabeth.

> E. The war with Spain and foreign involvement in plots increased the sense of danger.

> F. Elizabeth was under pressure from her councillors and Parliament to agree to Mary's execution.

2. There are different ways of organising the reasons for an event when writing an answer. We can divide the reasons into:

   a) long-term, short-term and immediate reasons (sometimes called 'triggers') for an event

   b) the most important and less important factors.

   Which method of organising the reasons for Mary's execution do you think will produce the most effective explanation? Explain your choice.

3. Choose one of the reasons on the cards above and write a full paragraph, using the evidence you chose in activity 1 and a connective to prove that the reason played a part in Mary's execution.

Visible Learning

Using connectives to improve your answer

When talking or writing about the reasons why Mary was executed, you cannot just **say** that a reason led to her execution. You have to **prove** that the reason played a part. One way to do this is using evidence – this is what activity 1, above, was about. In addition, you need to use **connectives** – the **golden words and phrases** in the Word Wall opposite, such as 'this meant that …', 'this led to …' and 'this increased the danger because …'.

We call these words and phrases **connectives** because they connect what you know to the question. They really help you to think, talk and write effectively when answering questions. You use them to:

- link your answer strongly to the question
- make your argument clear – for example, when writing about which factors were most important or explaining how factors were linked together
- show that there is evidence to prove your argument.

4.7 Communicating your answer

STOP

It's time to THINK about the answer

Now it is time to write a full answer to the question. If this were an examination, our enquiry question would look slightly different, even if it were the same question. It would say:

Explain why Mary, Queen of Scots was executed in 1587.

The guidance below will help you to complete your answer.

1. Revise your hypothesis and get your summary answer clear in your mind before you write. This is a really vital stage, because one of the biggest mistakes that students make is starting to write without having the answer clear in their mind.
2. Use your work from page 58 to decide how you will organise your answer – will you divide the reasons by importance, or into long, short and immediate reasons?
3. Decide what order to put the reasons in – one reason per paragraph.

You will find more guidance in the Writing Guide on pages 114–123.

And keep your Word Wall up to date

Here are some of the words from this chapter that will help you to write accurately and with confidence. Can you suggest other words to add to your wall?

'evil councillors'   double agent   custody   surveillance

political grievances   definitive   incriminate

'this meant that …',   'this led to …'   'this increased the danger because …'

Practice questions

1. Describe two features of:
   a) the Ridolfi Plot   **b)** the Babington Plot.
2. Explain why the Throckmorton Plot (1583) was a threat to Queen Elizabeth.
3. 'The Babington Plot was the main cause of the execution of Mary, Queen of Scots.' How far do you agree? Explain your answer.
4. 'Lack of foreign support was the main reason why Catholic revolts and plots against Elizabeth failed.' How far do you agree? Explain your answer.

You may use the following in your answer:
■ the Ridolfi Plot
■ the Bond of Association.
You **must** also use information of your own.

5.1 The Armada reappears

▲ A

B ▶

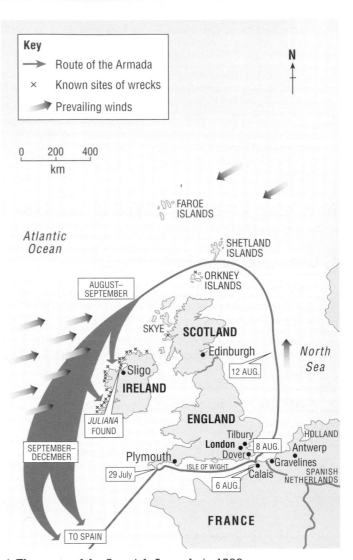

▲ The route of the Spanish Armada in 1588

In April 2015, following two years of winter storms, the remains of a ship were exposed on the seabed off the north-west coast of Ireland. After two months of work, archaeologists brought three bronze cannon ashore, still in excellent condition (see photo A). The engraving on the cannon of St Matorna, who had links with Barcelona, and the date 1570 enabled the ship to be identified as the *Juliana*, one of the ships sent by Philip II of Spain as part of the Spanish Armada.

The *Juliana* was one of three ships shipwrecked off this part of the coast of Ireland. The other two ships are believed to be still buried beneath the sands. They were just three of over 40 Spanish ships which sank off different parts of the west coast of Ireland, as the Spanish Armada tried to sail home following its battle with the English fleet at Gravelines, off the coast of the Netherlands.

The map above right shows the route the Spanish were forced to take. The winds in the English Channel (which typically blow from the south-west) prevented the Spanish fleet from turning round. Therefore, the Spanish sailors attempted to sail home to Spain around the British Isles, but the prevailing winds from across the Atlantic drove many of the ships onto rocks and sandbanks. Local Irish people killed many of the luckless sailors when they tried to land.

Elizabeth I wasted no time in producing propaganda to celebrate the English victory. Her government produced the Armada victory medal (see photo B) with the words, 'God blew and they were scattered'. Elizabeth gave credit for the defeat of the Armada to a Protestant God, who had caused the right winds to blow at the right time.

DEFEATING THE ARMADA   ❓

1. What reasons can you find in the text on this page for the defeat of the Armada?
2. Why do you think Elizabeth was so eager to give God credit for defeating the Armada?

5.2 Your enquiry: why did England and Spain go to war in 1585?

This chapter contains two enquiries. On pages 69–73 we will investigate why the Armada was defeated – was it really beaten just by the 'Protestant wind'? However, first we need to find out why Spain and England were at war at all. At the beginning of Elizabeth's reign, England and Spain were on friendly terms, so why did this change? The tasks below and two Knowledge Organisers – a continuum line in the form of a thermometer and a table – will help to structure your enquiry.

There are four possible causes of the outbreak of war:

■ **Religious rivalry** – Spain wanted to force England back to Catholicism
■ **Political rivalry** – Spain and England were rivals for power in Europe and the Americas
■ **Trade and commercial rivalry** – England was trying to take over Spanish trade in the Americas
■ **English direct involvement in the Netherlands** – Spain wanted to stop England interfering in the Spanish Netherlands, where Dutch Protestants were rebelling against Spanish control.

1. Creating your hypothesis

a) Draw your own copy of the thermometer. Write the four causes above on cards, then use pages 62–66 and what you have learned so far to place the four cards on the thermometer. These are first thoughts – you are not expected to be certain!

b) Write a paragraph answering the question, 'Why did England and Spain go to war in 1585?', using the position of the cards on the thermometer to guide you. This is your hypothesis.

2. Collecting the evidence for your judgements

The table below helps you to record the detailed evidence you need to justify where you place each of the cards on the thermometer. Here is how to use it:

a) Read about each cause of the war on pages 62–7. After you have read about a cause, fill in that section of your table. Use a large piece of paper (perhaps A3 size), so there is plenty of room for the evidence.

b) Use the evidence in your table to decide whether you wish to change your first thoughts on where that cause goes on the thermometer. If you do, revise your hypothesis paragraph. This keeps your answer to the question in your mind.

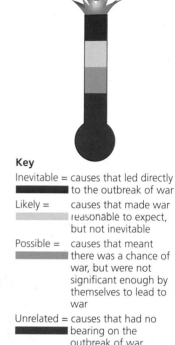

Key

Inevitable = causes that led directly to the outbreak of war

Likely = causes that made war reasonable to expect, but not inevitable

Possible = causes that meant there was a chance of war, but were not significant enough by themselves to lead to war

Unrelated = causes that had no bearing on the outbreak of war

▲ Path to war.

Visible learning

Language for discussing causes

When you answer 'Explain why …' questions, it is important that you think carefully about the words you use to describe how important a cause was – in this case, what role each cause played in the outbreak of war. The language of the criteria on the thermometer – words such as inevitable, likely, possible – provides clearer answers than more general statements, such as 'very important' or 'quite important'. Other words and phrases you could think about using about the roles of causes are:

key   crucial   essential   most influential
… played a significant/important/major role in …
… was of some importance in …

Cause	How did this cause increase the chances of war?	What limited the impact of this cause on the possibility of war?	Your judgement – what role did this cause play in the outbreak of war?
Religion			

Trade and commercial rivalry

It used to be thought that the main reason for the war was the commercial rivalry between England and Spain over trade to the **New World**. Before 1550, the bulk of English trade abroad was based on the export of woollen cloth to Antwerp, from where it was sold throughout Europe. Overproduction of woollen cloth led to a slump in the market in 1550, and when Spain began its campaign to bring the Netherlands under tighter control, the Antwerp market descended into chaos. Attempts to replace the cloth trade resulted in the establishment of some new markets overseas, with Elizabethan explorers travelling overland and setting up trading agreements with Russia and India.

A far more lucrative area, however, was the New World. The Spanish Empire there, consisting of Mexico, Peru, Chile and the Caribbean, offered opportunities to make money fast, either by attacking the Spanish treasure fleets or by trading with the **colonists**, who were short of many goods. Unfortunately for English explorers, this trade was illegal, because it required a licence from Spain, and Spain hardly ever gave licences to traders from other countries.

The activities, shown on the map opposite, therefore technically amounted to **piracy**, but the financial rewards were so great that Elizabeth pretended to know nothing about them, even though she unofficially supported these voyages in return for a share of the booty! Even the famous circumnavigation of the world by Francis Drake, described in detail in Chapter 7 (pages 98–101), included secret orders to attack the Spanish Empire whenever possible.

The main incidents, however, such as at San Juan de Ulua and Nombre de Dios, and the capture of the *Cacafuego* (see map opposite), took place years before war was declared. King Philip of Spain made many formal complaints about the activities of the English pirates, some of which Elizabeth acted on, but the chronology of these events shows that he did not go to war directly because of them.

Caca Fogo.

Caca Plata.

▲ The *Golden Hind* (right) attacking the *Cacafuego*, drawn in 1603.

TRADE AND COMMERCIAL RIVALRY ?

1. Using the information provided above and the map, explain:
   a) why trade and commercial rivalry could be seen as a major cause of war
   b) the arguments against this view
   c) the significance of using 'directly' in the last sentence above.

2. Now complete activity 2 on page 61 for this cause.

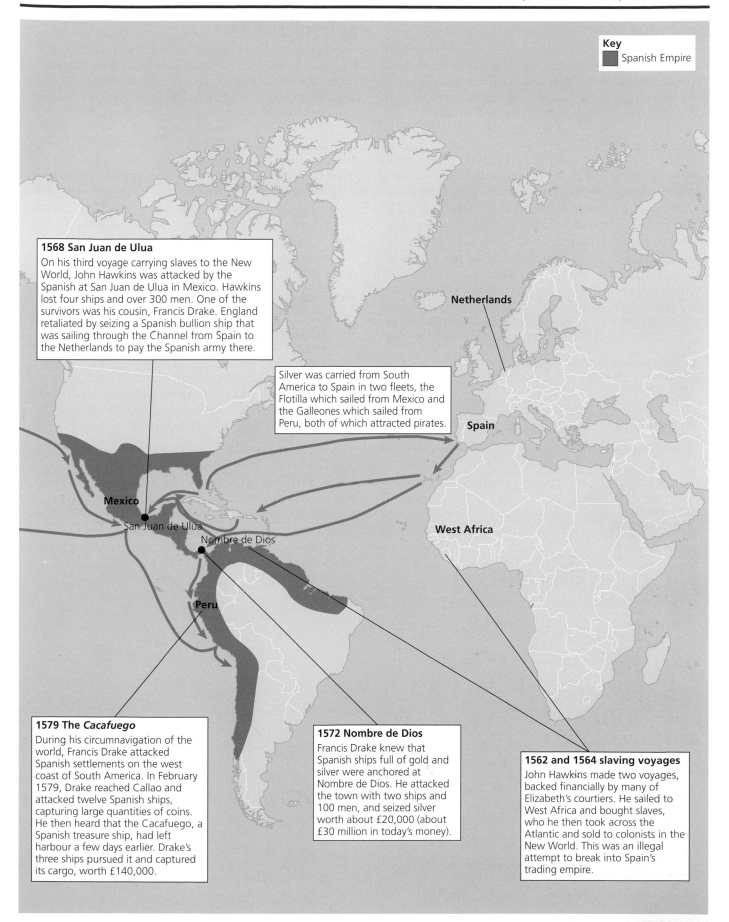

Key
Spanish Empire

1568 San Juan de Ulua
On his third voyage carrying slaves to the New World, John Hawkins was attacked by the Spanish at San Juan de Ulua in Mexico. Hawkins lost four ships and over 300 men. One of the survivors was his cousin, Francis Drake. England retaliated by seizing a Spanish bullion ship that was sailing through the Channel from Spain to the Netherlands to pay the Spanish army there.

Silver was carried from South America to Spain in two fleets, the Flotilla which sailed from Mexico and the Galleones which sailed from Peru, both of which attracted pirates.

Netherlands

Spain

West Africa

Mexico

San Juan de Ulua

Nombre de Dios

Peru

1579 The *Cacafuego*
During his circumnavigation of the world, Francis Drake attacked Spanish settlements on the west coast of South America. In February 1579, Drake reached Callao and attacked twelve Spanish ships, capturing large quantities of coins. He then heard that the Cacafuego, a Spanish treasure ship, had left harbour a few days earlier. Drake's three ships pursued it and captured its cargo, worth £140,000.

1572 Nombre de Dios
Francis Drake knew that Spanish ships full of gold and silver were anchored at Nombre de Dios. He attacked the town with two ships and 100 men, and seized silver worth about £20,000 (about £30 million in today's money).

1562 and 1564 slaving voyages
John Hawkins made two voyages, backed financially by many of Elizabeth's courtiers. He sailed to West Africa and bought slaves, who he then took across the Atlantic and sold to colonists in the New World. This was an illegal attempt to break into Spain's trading empire.

Religious rivalry

Another argument is that religion was the most important reason for the outbreak of war between England and Spain. The religious rivalry between the two countries was so great that it seemed to make war inevitable after Elizabeth set up a Protestant Church in 1559 and, from the 1570s onwards, began to increase penalties against Catholics (see page 56). When Catholic priests began arriving in England, this increased fears of a religious crusade (a holy war with a religious purpose, usually to recapture and convert lands). Philip II was certainly a devout Catholic, who saw it as his life's work to return countries to the Catholic Church. However, Philip took no action when Elizabeth created the Protestant Church of England, nor when the Pope excommunicated Elizabeth in 1571. He did not go to war because he did not want war with England at that time, as you can see explained in the diagram below. If religion was a cause of the outbreak of war, it was a long-term one. Philip had lived with a Protestant England for over 25 years.

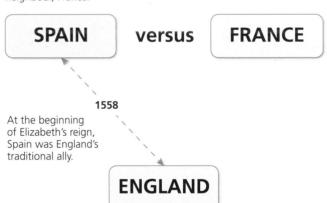

Spain was always worried about the threat from her neighbour, France.

SPAIN versus **FRANCE**

1558
At the beginning of Elizabeth's reign, Spain was England's traditional ally.

ENGLAND

England was not as powerful as France or Spain, but was useful to both of them. Philip was concerned that an attack on England would lead to France and England allying against Spain, and France had close links with Scotland.

Political rivalry

Another reason for the outbreak of war in 1585 is said to have been political rivalry. It is hard to separate religion and politics in the sixteenth century, because kings and queens, as well as ruling the country, were responsible for its religion. Philip II, apart from being a strong Catholic, was ruler of the most powerful country in the world. In addition to Spain itself, Philip ruled the Netherlands, an important trading country, and owned land in South America, the 'New World'. In 1580, he became King of Portugal as well. Treasure from the New World made Spain a very wealthy country and able to support a strong army and fleet. The activities of Francis Drake in the New World (see page 68), and the Earl of Leicester in the Netherlands (see page 66), were therefore seen by an angry Philip as direct interference in his affairs.

Philip did not want any other country to challenge Spanish power, but, certainly at first, he was more worried by France than England. Political rivalry does not seem to have been a major reason for the war. Philip's anxiety about the power of France meant that he preferred to have Elizabeth as Queen of England than Mary, Queen of Scots, who, although Catholic, had close ties with France. If Mary were Queen, he feared that an alliance between England and France would be much more likely.

This is why, although Spain was involved in the plots and rebellion to overthrow Elizabeth for Mary (see pages 50–55), Philip never did anything concrete, such as send an army. From Elizabeth's point of view, Spain's interference was a major source of irritation, but she reacted by expelling Spanish ambassadors rather than declaring war. Given the difference in the power of the two countries, it would have been a very brave or very foolish act for Elizabeth to declare war on Spain.

RELIGION AND WAR ?

1. Using the text and diagram above, and what you already know from Chapters 3 and 4, explain:
   a) why some historians have argued that religion was a cause of the outbreak of war between England and Spain
   b) the significance of the words 'seemed to' and 'long-term' in the text above
   c) how you would describe the importance of religion in the outbreak of war in 1585.

2. Now complete activity 2 on page 61 for this cause.

POLITICAL RIVALRY AND WAR

1. Using the information above and what you already know, explain:
   a) why political rivalry has been put forward as a cause of war
   b) the main arguments against this.

2. Now complete activity 2 on page 61 for this cause.

English direct involvement in the Netherlands

Most historians are now agreed that the war with Spain was caused by England's increasing involvement in the Netherlands, which was part of Spain's empire. The English Channel was vitally important to both Elizabeth and Philip, for trade, security and, in Philip's case, access to his territories in the Netherlands (see map).

In 1572, Protestants in the Netherlands rebelled against Spanish rule. The Dutch rebels asked their fellow-Protestant Elizabeth for help when Philip II sent a huge Spanish army against them. As the diagram at the top of page 66 shows, this created a problem for Elizabeth, as her favourite, Robert Dudley, Earl of Leicester, and others argued for sending major help to the Dutch Protestants.

▶ The importance of the English Channel to both England and Spain.

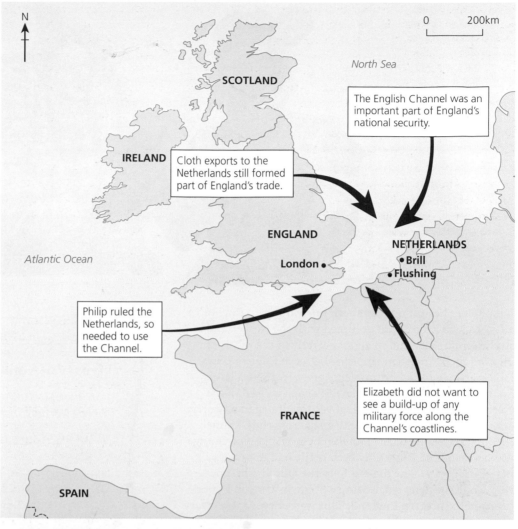

The English Channel was an important part of England's national security.

Cloth exports to the Netherlands still formed part of England's trade.

Philip ruled the Netherlands, so needed to use the Channel.

Elizabeth did not want to see a build-up of any military force along the Channel's coastlines.

◀ Robert Dudley, Earl of Leicester, painted c.1575 by an unknown artist.

Should England intervene directly in the Netherlands?

We need to help our fellow Protestants. Spanish victory will extend the power of Catholics in Europe and leave England isolated.

If the Dutch rebels are defeated, Spain will increase its power along the Channel coastline and be a threat to England.

Sending an army to the Netherlands would be very expensive.

It is best if things stay as they are. Once Catholic armies start arriving in Holland, who knows what the outcome will be. If France gets involved, too, it will be even worse for us.

Despite her hesitation, Elizabeth knew it was to England's advantage to keep Spain occupied with the Netherlands, so she sent money and weapons secretly to the rebels and allowed them and their ships to shelter in English ports. However, over time, the problems grew. In 1578, a larger Spanish army, led by the Duke of Parma, arrived in the Netherlands, and the English government began to worry about the presence of this army just across the Channel. In 1584, the leader of the Dutch rebels, William of Orange, was assassinated. Now Elizabeth really had to make a major decision. If she did not help the Dutch rebels now, they would be defeated, leaving a Spanish army in a good position to threaten England. This was when, in the Treaty of Nonsuch (see scroll), Elizabeth finally agreed to direct involvement in the Netherlands, and sent an army led by the Earl of Leicester. Spanish and English armies were now facing each other and the two countries were at war.

Elizabeth's cautious orders to Leicester were to keep Spain from overwhelming the Netherlands completely. Despite this, Philip II saw Leicester's arrival in the Netherlands as an act of war against Spain. From 1585, although there had been no formal declaration, both Philip and Elizabeth considered Spain and England at war. The arrival of Leicester boosted Dutch spirits, but the campaign was not a great success. Leicester felt that Elizabeth was not providing enough money or equipment, and he quarrelled with both his officers and his Dutch allies. Elizabeth, meanwhile, was horrified at the cost of the campaign. She was also furious when Leicester accepted the title of 'Governor General of the Low Countries'. This implied that England wanted some control over the Netherlands and Elizabeth believed, rightly, that this would enrage Spain even more. The presence of the English army did, however, slow down the advance of the Spanish army under the Duke of Parma, and prevented him from capturing the deep-water port of Flushing.

Treaty of Nonsuch, August 1585

Elizabeth to take over the protection of the Netherlands

An army of 7,000 to be sent to help the rebels

England to pay for the costs of this army

In exchange for this assistance, the Netherlands was to allow Elizabeth to use Brill and Flushing as bases for English soldiers.

ENGLISH DIRECT INVOLVEMENT IN THE NETHERLANDS ❓

1. Using the information above, explain:
   a) why English involvement in the Netherlands is thought to be the main cause of the war
   b) whether you can suggest links between English direct involvement in the Netherlands and any of the other causes.

2. Now complete activity 2 on page 61 for this cause.

5.3 Communicating your answer

It is time to write your answer to our question, which, in an examination, might well appear like this:

Explain why war broke out between England and Spain in 1585.

As before, you need to have your answer clear in your mind before you start writing.

1. Return to your completed thermometer from page 61. Check that you are happy with where you have placed each cause.

2. In addition to identifying the role of each cause, it is helpful to think about how they were linked – making war more likely to break out. In Philip II's mind, they must have felt connected. Draw the diagram below (without the street-criers!), then:

    a) draw lines between causes that you think were interconnected

    b) annotate your diagram to explain those connections.

3. Now use your thermometer, chart and completed diagram to revise your hypothesis paragraph for the last time. This will make sure that you have a clear answer to the question.

4. The text on pages 62–66 provides examples you can use in your answer.

    a) Connectives were used to tie each reason to the question. These included:

    > another argument is   another reason for
    > does not seem a major reason for

    b) Each cause was supported by historical detail, so that it was not just opinion with no evidence.

    c) Each cause was analysed in terms of the role it played in the outbreak of war, explaining which causes were more significant than others.

    Now it is time to write your answer!

5.4 Why was the Armada defeated?

On pages 68–74, you are going to investigate the question above, but this time we are not going to give you detailed help with structuring your research. It is important to develop the ability to work independently, as this will help you if you go on to A levels and beyond. However, we have given you plenty of help in the past that you can re-use. For example, look back at the overall plan of how to undertake an enquiry on page 18, and at the structure of the last enquiry on why war broke out. Here are two tasks to get you thinking about how to tackle this enquiry:

1. Use your past work to create a plan for your enquiry. For example, think about which Knowledge Organisers will help with this causation question.
2. Start thinking about the question and answer straightaway. What reasons can you think of which might explain the defeat of the Armada?
   a) Look back to page 60 for ideas
   b) Think about other wars you have studied and why one side won and one side lost.

Now begin your enquiry. Good luck!

> On pages 68–74, you will see questions in boxes like this. These are questions to prompt your thinking, not formal tasks that structure your enquiry. That is your job!

The beginnings of the Armada

Elizabeth used the three years between the outbreak of war in 1585 and the sailing of the Armada in 1588 to strengthen England's defences. Every county was ordered to provide soldiers to defend the coast, **warning beacons** were set up, and trading ships were converted into fighting ships.

In addition, as soon as war broke out, and perhaps aware of the drain on government finances that this would bring, Elizabeth put Francis Drake in charge of an expedition to attack the lucrative Spanish West Indies. He sailed in 1585, with about 30 ships and 2,300 men. Not everything went to plan. Drake missed the opportunity to attack the Spanish treasure fleet, and his raids in the Caribbean caused him heavy casualties, some due to disease. He did, however, capture two wealthy towns, so that he returned home to England with treasure worth £30,000.

This expedition helped to convince Philip that he could not put up with this drain on Spain's finances, or continue to be humiliated by Drake, *El Draque* (the Dragon), and he speeded up his plans to deal with England once and for all. Robert Hutchinson, in *Elizabeth's Spymaster* (2007), believed that Drake's expedition was one of the two main causes of the Armada.

> Many believe the execution of Mary, Queen of Scots, triggered, or at least accelerated, King Philip II of Spain's … plan to assault England. In truth, the genesis of the invasion was more the anger caused in 1585 by Francis Drake's plundering, burning voyage to the West Indies and Leicester's expedition to the Low Countries [Netherlands].

> **Elizabeth's government**
> The government of Elizabeth I's reign was not what we would mean today by 'the government'. Elizabeth's government usually refers to her councillors, chosen by her and not elected.

Drake and the raid on Cadiz

When news of Philip's assembling of a great fleet reached England, Francis Drake persuaded the Queen that attack was the best form of defence. In April 1587, with a small but carefully selected group of ships, he set sail to weaken Spain's preparations for war. In a cheeky and daring raid, he sailed into Cadiz harbour in Spain, avoiding its forts and guns, and inflicted heavy damage on the Spanish ships anchored there. This act, known in England, though not in Spain, as 'the singeing of the King of Spain's beard', delayed the construction of the Armada by destroying ships and supplies and then diverting Spanish warships in pursuit of Drake. After the attack on Cadiz, Drake's convoy sailed northwards, destroying local Portuguese vessels heading for Lisbon with materials needed for making the barrels that would hold the Armada's food supplies. Finally, Drake headed off to the Azores, where his men captured a Spanish treasure ship, the *San Felipe*, returning home to England with £114,000. His actions left the Spanish admirals in confusion and dread, and bought Elizabeth another twelve months to prepare England's defences.

> What was so important about Drake's raid on Cadiz in 1587?

SEIZURE OF SPANISH TREASURE-SHIPS BY DRAKE.

▲ This wood-engraving by W.B. Gardner commemorates Francis Drake's 1587 raid on Cadiz harbour, when he 'singed the King of Spain's beard' by inflicting heavy damage on the Spanish fleet that was being assembled there, and delayed the sailing of the Armada for twelve months.

The Spanish plan

It is easy to assume that the Spanish plan for the Armada was for the Spanish ships to sail directly to the English coast and then for Spanish soldiers to go ashore and invade England. This was NOT the plan! The real plan is set out in the map below.

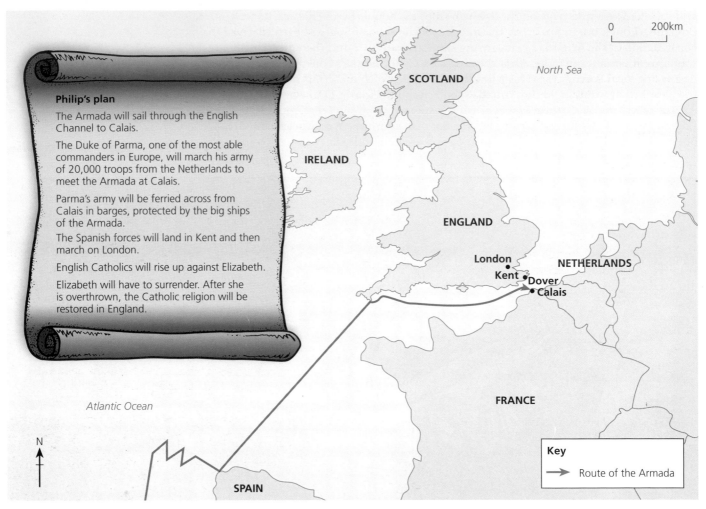

Philip's plan

The Armada will sail through the English Channel to Calais.

The Duke of Parma, one of the most able commanders in Europe, will march his army of 20,000 troops from the Netherlands to meet the Armada at Calais.

Parma's army will be ferried across from Calais in barges, protected by the big ships of the Armada.

The Spanish forces will land in Kent and then march on London.

English Catholics will rise up against Elizabeth.

Elizabeth will have to surrender. After she is overthrown, the Catholic religion will be restored in England.

Key

→ Route of the Armada

▲ 130 Spanish ships, carrying 17,000 men, sailed up the Channel to rendezvous with the Spanish army, under the Duke of Parma, in the Netherlands.

1. What possible unknowns or weaknesses can you see in the Spanish plan?
2. Did these weaknesses mean the Armada was doomed from the start?

The first critical problem in the plan was how the ships of the Armada and Parma's army were going to link up. This required good communications between the ships – which were at sea – and Parma, so that his troops would be ready when the Armada arrived. However, Parma's army could not be at Calais too soon, because their barges could easily be attacked by Dutch pirates. The timing had to be spot-on. It was not. Francisco de Bobadillo, the Spanish general in charge of the soldiers on board the Armada, wrote in September 1588:

> Medina Sidonia managed to bring his fleet to anchor in Calais. If on the day that we had arrived there, Parma had come out with his troops, we should have carried out the invasion.

The sailor and courtier, Sir Walter Raleigh, later criticised the Spanish plan, saying:

> To invade by sea, on a perilous coast, being neither in possession of any port, nor with any allies, may better fit a prince presuming (relying) on his fortune than enriched with understanding.

This view was reinforced 300 years later by the historian, Felipe Fernández-Armesto:

> If there was a critical omission from the Spanish plan, it was probably the lack of a secure port in northern waters.

Tactics

On 21 July 1588, 130 Spanish ships, carrying 17,000 men, sailed up the English Channel in a crescent formation, aiming for Calais to meet up with the Spanish army under the Duke of Parma, currently in the Netherlands. The English fleet left harbour in Plymouth and followed the Armada for eight days. The English navy had slightly more ships than the Spanish fleet, and had quicker ships with longer-range guns. The English fleet aimed to destroy the Spanish ships from a distance by firing cannon at them, but in those eight days the English ships failed to inflict serious damage on the Armada.

Philip had instructed his commander to get close enough to the enemy's ships for the Spanish sailors to board them and then capture them, but this was not possible because the English kept their distance. Despite this, on 6 August, the Spanish ships reached Calais harbour and dropped anchor. The first stage of the Spanish plan seemed to have been successful.

During the night, the English commander, Lord Howard, decided to go on the offensive. He ordered that eight unmanned English ships be filled with inflammable materials such as tar and gunpowder. At around midnight, these ships were set on fire and the winds carried them towards the Spanish ships in the harbour. The sight of these fireships coming towards them caused panic among the Spanish sailors, who pulled up or cut their anchors, losing their tight battle formation. The Armada was blown towards the coast of the Netherlands.

They were eight vessels with sails set, which were drifting towards our flagship and the rest of the Armada, all of them burning with great fury. When I saw them approaching, fearful that they might contain fire machines or mines, I ordered the flagship to let go the cables, the rest of the Armada receiving similar orders, with an indication that when the fires had passed they were to return to the same positions again. The current was so strong that most of the ships of the Armada were carried towards Dunkirk.

Duke of Medina Sidonia, Commander of the Armada, 7 August 1588

The result of the fireships being used was that the Armada was scattered and was no longer in a position to link up with Parma's army. The loss of their anchors also made it impossible to take shelter in harbours.

At daylight on 8 August, Lord Howard gave the order to attack. The battle of Gravelines lasted for most of the day and was fought in very poor weather conditions, with rough seas and bad visibility. Many of the Spanish ships were damaged or lost, and 1,000 sailors were killed. No English ships were lost and about 50 English sailors lost their lives.

> 1. Identify other possible causes of the defeat that are linked to the tactics the two fleets used.
> 2. From what you have read so far, did the Armada fail because of Spanish failings or English strengths?

▲ The fireships attacking the Armada in Calais harbour, painted in the early seventeenth century by a Dutch artist, Aert van Antum.

I sent my fleet against men, not against the wind and the waves. *Philip II, 1588*

▲ The words on this medal, made soon after the defeat of the Armada in 1588, mean, 'God blew and they were scattered'.

▼ Spanish wrecks off the coasts of Scotland and Ireland. Each cross indicates the known site of a wreck.

The most widespread contemporary analysis of the Armada's failure – winds – seems justified. *Felipe Fernández-Armesto, The Spanish Armada, 1988*

The wind and weather

As you read on page 60, in the introduction to this chapter, Elizabeth and her government claimed that God sent the 'Protestant wind' to defeat the Armada. How much truth was there in this claim?

The impact of the fireships and the battle of Gravelines had seriously damaged the Spanish ships. The next day, the wind changed direction, forcing the Spanish fleet out into the North Sea, so they tried to make their way back to Spain around Scotland and Ireland. The English gave chase for a while, but as they were running short of supplies, they decided to turn back. Over 40 Spanish ships were wrecked off the coasts of Scotland and Ireland (see map), with thousands of sailors either drowned or killed by the local inhabitants. Only about 80 ships struggled back to Spanish ports by the end of the year. The unseasonal English weather played a key role in the Armada's defeat, from the steady breeze that blew the fireships towards Calais, to the winds that drove the Armada northwards around the British Isles, to the storms that scattered and wrecked their ships on the coasts of Ireland and Scotland.

What had the Spanish done when attacked by the fireships that made their voyage much more dangerous?

The quality of leadership

Does Elizabeth deserve her successful reputation for leading England to victory against the Armada? Once the Armada was in the Channel, she could not affect events or tactics, but her commanders, Howard, Drake and Hawkins, did know what had to be done. It was her Admiral and overall commander, Lord Howard, who ordered the sending of fireships. Elizabeth had picked the right men for the job.

Eleven days after the battle of Gravelines, Elizabeth appeared before troops still stationed at Tilbury, dressed in a helmet and armour, to deliver probably her most famous speech:

> I know I have the body of a weak and feeble woman, but I have the heart and stomach of a king and a King of England too, and think foul scorn that Parma or Spain, or any Prince of Europe, should dare to invade the borders of my realm.

Once again, Elizabeth had created the image of the powerful leader, Gloriana, this time standing shoulder to shoulder with her ordinary subjects to defy the most powerful empire in Europe; an image which would remain long after 1588.

Philip appointed the Duke of Medina Sidonia as his commander of the Armada, after his first choice died in 1587. He did not have a naval background and asked to be excused from the position as he suffered from seasickness. Once at sea, he proved to be a brave leader, but was hampered throughout by his orders from Philip II, as Paul Hammer explains in *Elizabeth's Wars* (2003):

> The central element of Philip's plan – the junction of the Armada and Parma's army – was impractical from the outset, but Medina Sidonia's restrictive instructions and lack of naval experience, coupled with vigorous enemy counter-attack and inclement weather, ensured there was no realistic possibility of improvising a viable alternative.

When the Spanish commander ordered his fleet to anchor off Calais in a final effort to meet up with Parma, the Armada was an easy target.

FRANCIS DRAKE, 1543–96

▲ The son of a well-off Devon farmer who gained fame as a sailor and Protestant preacher.

1571–2: led expeditions to plunder Mexico and Peru in the Spanish New World

1577–80: circumnavigated the world, capturing the treasure ship *Cacafuego* and attacking Spanish colonies; knighted by the Queen on his return

1585: led the attack on the Spanish West Indies as the Queen's Admiral

1587: 'singed the King of Spain's beard' by his attack on the Spanish fleet in Cadiz, and then captured the wealthy *San Felipe*

1588: Vice Admiral of the fleet which defeated the Armada

1. When exactly does leadership seem to have been important during the events of the Armada?
2. Why would it have been difficult for a single leader, on either side, to inspire his men?

LORD CHARLES HOWARD OF EFFINGHAM, 1ST EARL OF NOTTINGHAM, 1536–1624

▲ Followed the traditional route to promotion for a noble under Elizabeth, as a courtier and MP, and so had a less spectacular career than Drake and Hawkins.

1570: commanded a squadron of ships that escorted the Queen of Spain on a state visit

1573: became the first Earl of Nottingham

1585: made **Lord High Admiral** by Elizabeth

1588: commanded all the forces at sea against the Armada and, with Drake, was considered responsible for England's victory

JOHN HAWKINS, 1532–95

▲ A renowned navigator and early slave trader

1578: appointed Treasurer and **Comptroller** of the English navy; set about redesigning English ships to make them more streamlined

1588: naval commander against the Armada

Resources

The strength of the two sides was fairly evenly matched, but where there were differences, the advantage tended to lie with England, as this chart shows.

> At what stage of events did the differences between the resources of the two sides matter most?

	English	Spanish	The winner
Ships	54 battleships and 140 merchant ships that had been converted	64 battleships, including 22 huge galleons, and 45 converted merchant ships, plus about 20 store ships	The Spanish ships were slower and harder to manoeuvre than the English ones. John Hawkins had designed a new type of English battleship, which was faster and lower. The tall and heavy Spanish galleons could not deal with the new-style English ships nipping in between them and were easy targets.
Weapons	Nearly 2,000 cannon and smaller guns	2,000 cannon	Spanish cannon were heavier than the English and with shorter range. They were designed to fire once, after which it was expected that the Spanish forces would board the enemy ship. The English guns could fire consecutively. This explains why the English were able to inflict so much damage when they got among the Spanish ships at Gravelines.
Forces at sea	14,000 sailors	30,000 men, of which 8,000 were experienced sailors, 19,000 were trained soldiers and the remainder were servants and priests	Admirals on both sides were experienced sea captains, although the majority of Spanish sailors were more used to the calmer waters of the Mediterranean.
Forces on land	20,000 soldiers, with three main armies placed at Tilbury, Essex and Kent	About 20,000 (the Duke of Parma's army waiting in the Netherlands)	England did not have a permanent, regular army, but all able-bodied men received annual training in case they were called up to fight. Parma's army was the best-equipped and best-trained in Europe, with 'crack units', but when the Armada anchored at Calais, Parma's army was still a week's march away, held up by Dutch rebels at Dunkirk.

5.5 Communicating your answer

By now, you have completed your research and built up an answer. Use the guidance on pages 67 and 68 to help you write your answer to the following question:

Explain why the Spanish Armada was defeated.

Remember to update your Word Wall. Some suggestions follow below.

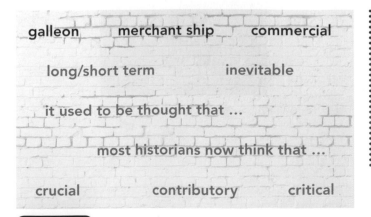

galleon   merchant ship   commercial

long/short term   inevitable

it used to be thought that ...

most historians now think that ...

crucial   contributory   critical

> ### Practice questions
> 1. Describe two features of:
>   a) Drake's attacks on Spanish shipping and trade
>   b) the English navy sent against the Spanish Armada
>   c) the naval battle off Gravelines.
> 2. 'Religious rivalry rather than commercial or political rivalry caused the war between Spain and England.' How far do you agree? Explain your answer.

Challenges to Elizabeth at home and abroad, 1569–88: review

Now you have studied all the challenges, we must return to the central theme of the book:

Does Elizabeth deserve her successful reputation?

Remember the conversations you heard on pages 14–15.

> Another queen! She won't be able to rule on her own.

> Catholics will be angry. There could be a rebellion.

> It would be clever of Elizabeth to marry King Philip of Spain.

1. What would they have thought?

In a group, rewrite conversations between these people, as if they were taking place in 1588, after the defeat of the Armada. You can write much longer conversations to build in more complex ideas. Think about the following:

- Would they all agree that Elizabeth dealt well with the plots and revolt?
- Would they have seen her religious decisions as a success or a cause of danger?
- Would they agree on the causes of the war with Spain?
- Would they believe Elizabeth was responsible for the defeat of the Armada?
- Would they think Elizabeth had been a great success?

2. The scales of reputation!

Which events and actions during these years would you place on the scales you can see to the right? The cards below identify some of the events that could be placed on one side or the other.

1. Which cards would you put on each side?
2. Write a short answer to the following question: 'The events of 1569–88 show that Elizabeth's successful reputation was fully justified.' How far do you agree? Explain your answer.

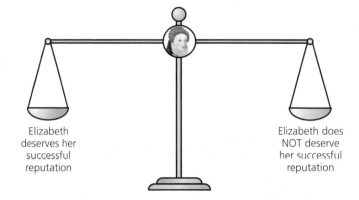

Elizabeth deserves her successful reputation

Elizabeth does NOT deserve her successful reputation

The defeat of the Armada	Delaying decisions about whether to execute Mary	Failure to marry	Catholic rebellions and plots	The roles of Howard, Drake and Hawkins during the Armada
Sending an army to the Netherlands	Executing Mary	Catholics did not rebel when the Armada arrived	The work of Cecil and Walsingham to protect Elizabeth	The weather in 1588

Visible learning: revise and remember

1. Recording and assessing the role of an individual

During your course, you will learn about the roles a variety of individuals played during Elizabeth's reign. It will be much easier to revise their achievements and write about them in exams if you use the same kind of chart for each one. This will mean the pattern of the chart will be clear in your mind when you need it. The headings in the chart below will help you create charts for all the major individuals you study, although you will have to change the pronouns for women! Do not be afraid to think for yourself and vary the chart for different individuals, so you record the most important information.

Francis Drake
Dates of birth and death, titles and positions held

Activities: which events was he involved with?	Assessment: did he make Elizabeth's reign more effective or more difficult?
The most interesting thing you have learned about him:	The two most important things you need to remember about him:

2. Assessing the dangers to Elizabeth

In Chapters 4 and 5, you have investigated the challenges facing Elizabeth at home and abroad between 1569 and 1588. Elizabeth, however, did not have the luxury of dealing with the two challenges separately, and in any case, they were not separate problems.

Complete a 'living graph' like the one below for the years 1569–88. Use Chapters 4–5 and your notes to place on the graph each year in which there was a major event. For example, if 1569 was a year of crisis and you think Elizabeth was fearful, write 1569 at the bottom of the graph.

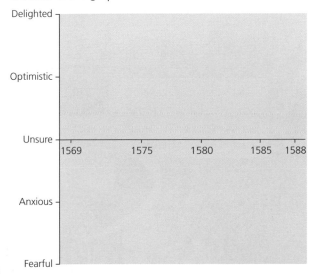

3. Creating mnemonics

The drawing illustrates the sentence

White **l**amb **p**lays **t**he **r**ecorder

The initial letters help you to remember the key features of a topic. In this case, the initial letters stand for the reasons why the Armada failed, beginning with **W**ind and **L**eadership.

1. What do the other initial letters stand for?
2. Create a mnemonic to help you remember the rebellions and plots against Elizabeth.
3. What other topics could a mnemonic help with?

4. Set questions yourself

Work in a group of three. Each of you should set four revision questions on the topics in Chapters 4 and 5. Use the style of questions above. Then ask each other the questions – and make sure you know the answers to the questions that you have set!

5. Test yourself!

The more you think about what you have learned, and **especially what you are not sure about**, the more chance you have of succeeding in your exam. So answer these questions and do not be surprised if we ask you these questions again.

1. When was the Revolt of the Northern Earls and who led it?	**2.** Give two reasons for the outbreak of war between England and Spain in 1585.	**3.** What happened at Cadiz in 1587?
4. When was Mary, Queen of Scots executed?	**5.** What was important about the 1570 Papal Bull of Excommunication?	**6.** What happened in Paris in 1572?
7. Who commanded the Spanish Armada and the English fleet sent against it?	**8.** Who began arriving in England in 1574?	**9.** Give two examples to show how worried Parliament was for Elizabeth's safety.
10. What happened at Gravelines in 1588?	**11.** Explain what the Throckmorton Plot of 1583 was and why it failed.	**12.** List three ways in which Walsingham's 'secret service' protected Elizabeth.
13. List three reasons for the defeat of the Spanish Armada in 1588.	**14.** What did you find hardest to understand in this section? How are you going to help yourself to understand it?	**15.** Name one thing that you learned in this section that surprised you or that you now think differently about. Explain why.

Elizabethan society in the age of exploration, 1558–88

Moments in time: 1588 – Elizabeth's Golden Age?

Elizabeth's reign is often said to be a 'Golden Age', a time when people were more prosperous and happier, when new and important events were taking place. Key topic 3 is going to examine the idea that this was really a Golden Age. This illustration of London in 1588 introduces the issues we will be exploring in Chapters 6 and 7.

A GOLDEN AGE?

Read the conversations taking place in the picture.

1. Make a list of events or issues which:
   a) support the idea that Elizabeth's reign was a Golden Age
   b) challenge the idea of a Golden Age.
2. Which of these achievements and problems do you think can be directly credited to the Queen?
3. What questions do you want to ask about the topics mentioned in the conversations?

This chapter investigates four topics that the people on the last page were talking about – you can see them below. Each one has a statement next to it. Your challenge is to test the four statements and decide whether the evidence supports or challenges the statement.

- **Leisure** – There were plenty of opportunities to enjoy life when you were not working (pages 82–85).
- **Education** – The opportunities for better education increased during Elizabeth's reign (pages 86–87).
- **Poverty** – Fewer people were poor during Elizabeth's reign (pages 88–89).
- **Attitudes to the poor** – Elizabeth's government tried hard to help everyone who was poor (pages 90–91).

When you test each statement, the simplest way to collect evidence is in a Knowledge Organiser, such as this chart:

Evidence supporting the statement	Evidence challenging the statement

6.1 More comfortable lives?

In the 1570s, a churchman from Essex called William Harrison travelled round the country to find out about the lives of the people. He wrote a book called *The Description of England*, which was published in 1577. Harrison's book gives us a lot of information about everyday life. For example, he describes how people at the time divided the population into four classes:

Gentlemen: nobles, lords and gentry

Citizens and burgesses in the towns: merchants, master craftsmen and lawyers

Yeomen: farmers who owned their own land

The fourth sort: farm labourers, servants, shopkeepers and craftspeople, such as tailors, shoemakers, carpenters and bricklayers

A

► One way Elizabethan nobles showed their wealth was to have grand houses built. Burghley House, shown here, was built in Lincolnshire for William Cecil, Lord Burghley, between 1552 and 1589. He also had two other large houses built for himself, one in London and one in Hertfordshire.

'The fourth sort' was the class most people belonged to and also included the poor and the unemployed. These are the people it is hardest to find out about. Their homes and possessions have not survived and few of them could read or write. Our evidence about the 'fourth sort' often depends largely on what the other social groups said about them.

In Elizabeth's reign, there were many opportunities for the better-off to increase their wealth and social status through education, buying land, moving into trade and commerce, following a career at court or in local government, or even marrying into the class above. These people were able to provide a comfortable life for themselves and their families.

William Harrison provides plenty of information in his book about changes that had taken place in recent years. He spoke to older people who said that, by the 1570s, people were living much more comfortably than 40 or 50 years earlier. Here is a summary of some of the things Harrison recorded.

> More houses are being built of stone and brick, though most are still built of wood. They have fireplaces and chimneys, and glass in their windows.
>
> Many houses have many rooms on several floors, and oak panels on the walls to keep them warm. Tapestries and painted cloths are also hung on walls.
>
> Everyone has more furniture, and they have cups, plates and spoons made of silver and pewter, instead of wood. They sleep on feather mattresses, not straw, and place pillows, not logs, under their heads at night.

> The inventory of John Lawson of Chester, who died in 1580, tells us more about the standard of living of Elizabethan people. He was comfortably off, although not rich, but still managed to leave behind items which included an iron fireplace, a dining table with a carpet, wooden chests, stools, cushions, bedsteads with mattresses, pillows and wall hangings, pewter plates and dishes, brass pots and silver spoons.

CHANGING TIMES?

1. What evidence in pictures A and B supports Harrison's statements?

2. Which details in John Lawson's inventory:
   a) support Harrison's statements?
   b) add new information to Harrison's statements?

▼ A restored Elizabethan yeoman's home.

6.2 Sport, pastimes and the theatre

YOUR CHALLENGE

The pictures and descriptions on pages 82–3 provide you with evidence of the many pastimes enjoyed by people in Elizabeth's reign. Use them to complete the tasks below.

1. On your own copy of the Venn diagram, write in the pastimes enjoyed by the different groups of people.

2. Use a chart such as the one on page 80 to collect evidence which supports or challenges the following statement:

   There were plenty of opportunities to enjoy life when you were not working.

3. Write a paragraph developing or correcting the statement above, using the evidence in your chart.

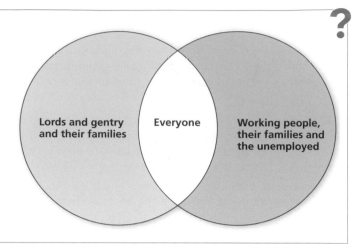

Lords and gentry and their families — Everyone — Working people, their families and the unemployed

▲ Inns and taverns were an important part of everyday life for the lower classes; ale was even drunk at breakfast.

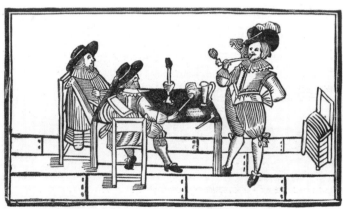

▲ Tobacco was becoming increasingly popular, but it was still expensive – a treat for when money was not so scarce.

▲ Gambling on the outcome of sports such as bear-baiting, cock-fighting and racing, as well as cards and dice, held out the promise of an easy win, particularly among the poorest classes.

▲ Celebrating feast days, such as Saints' Days, May Day and Plough Monday, offered an opportunity for dancing and drinking in the village.

▲ Archery and fishing were popular at all levels of society. 'The fourth sort' also took part in wrestling, running and football. Gentlemen preferred fencing, tennis and bowls.

▲ Storytelling played an important part in the lives of the ordinary people. The invention of the printing press led to popular stories like Robin Hood being published for a new mass market, although gentlemen were more likely to line their shelves with translations of famous Greek and Roman texts. The theatres which gentlemen attended were also attended by the 'fourth sort'.

▲ All classes took part in hunting. For the upper classes, this was preferably for deer, but hawking came a close second. 'The fourth sort' were more likely to hunt rabbit.

▲ Nobles employed household musicians, while the gentry bought madrigal songbooks and organised musical evenings. 'The fourth sort' sang ballads, often adding their own words to tunes composed in London.

'The fourth sort'
We have used Harrison's phrase in these captions to include both working people and the unemployed.

Going to the theatre

The first theatres were built in Britain by the Romans, but after they left, the theatres were abandoned and there were no more built for about a thousand years. Going to watch plays, however, continued as a popular form of entertainment. Groups of actors travelled around the country, together with acrobats, jugglers and minstrels. They performed stories from the Bible and miracle plays on temporary platforms, in marketplaces and inn yards.

There was not a single theatre in the country when Elizabeth became Queen. Many local authorities thought that groups of travelling actors were a threat to law and order and should be punished as vagabonds. In London, however, some powerful nobles, like the Earl of Leicester, protected groups of actors, giving financial and legal support, and ensured their plays continued to be performed to the city's growing population. Wealthy traders and manufacturers who lived in London, and their workers, had the money to watch plays. Against this background, the first theatre to be built since Roman times opened just outside London in 1576. It was built by James Burbage, and called the Theatre, and was such a success that it was soon followed by the Curtain in 1577 and the Rose in 1587. The most famous theatre, Shakespeare's Globe, came later, in 1599.

People from all social classes loved the theatre. Entrance fees were cheap; for one penny, the audience could stand in the pit. These 'groundlings' were very close to the actors and were known for being noisy. They also got very wet if it rained during a performance. For two or three pennies, wealthier spectators could stand or sit in one of the three covered galleries. The upper classes sat on stools on the stage, presumably as much to be seen as to see.

Elizabethan playwrights wrote some of the most popular and acclaimed plays ever written. Audiences appreciated the complex characters, gripping plots and memorable lines delivered in blank verse by imposing actors of the day, like Richard Burbage and Edward Allen. Christopher Marlowe was the first famous Elizabethan playwright. In Marlowe's *The Jew of Malta*, the wealth of Barabas, the richest man on the island, is seized, and he schemes to regain it until his death at the hands of Maltese soldiers. The play crackles with religious conflict, intrigue and revenge, and is also considered to be the first successful black comedy. Elizabethan audiences loved it.

Some Elizabethans, however, opposed the theatre. They thought it would encourage idleness, spread disease and create unrest. Puritans believed that theatres were the work of the Devil. The Lord Mayor of London asked the Privy Council to control the theatres, but the councillors only seemed prepared to close them down when plague was a threat.

The Queen did not go to the theatre, but she invited actors to Court to perform their plays for her. She obviously enjoyed the plays; in 1572, there is a record showing that she added a tip of around £3 to the payment due to the Lord Chamberlain's Men for a play presented at Court on St Stephen's Day. However, the Queen, too, was worried that theatre audiences might hear religious or political messages that criticised her government. In 1572, censorship was introduced. All acting companies had to have a royal licence, and all play scripts had to be submitted to the Master of Revels, who was responsible for co-ordinating all theatrical entertainment at Court, before they were performed.

WHAT ABOUT SHAKESPEARE?

William Shakespeare is by far the most famous playwright of this time, but he is not mentioned above. This is because he wrote his first play around 1591, and your course ends in 1588! So if you are asked about theatres and writers in your exam, then writing about Shakespeare will not be relevant. However, Shakespeare could not have been a success, and there would have been no theatres for him to work in, if it had not been for the growth in theatres from the 1570s. The success of his plays shows that theatres were thriving by the 1580s.

ELIZABETHAN THEATRE ?

1. Describe two features of theatres in Elizabethan London.

2. What made going to the theatre so popular?

3. What was Elizabeth's attitude to theatres and plays?

▲ Early Elizabethan theatres were lively places. The audience wandered around during performances, eating and drinking, and made their opinions of the plays clear through clapping, booing and even throwing things at the actors. The playwrights were not often university graduates, and the plays could be coarse and rowdy, which perhaps accounts for their popularity. In addition, theatres were expected to put on a new play every couple of days, so there was little time for rehearsal. Most of these 600 or so plays from this period no longer remain. One which does, Udall's *Ralph Roister Doister*, combined the style of classical playwrights like Seneca with the more English themes of chivalry. It is often regarded as the first English comedy and influenced other writers, including Shakespeare. Elizabethan audiences clearly loved plots with action, excitement and humour. There was no scenery, so people could focus on the play, but the actors did wear colourful costumes. Acting was not considered suitable for a woman, so the female parts were played by young boys. Performances took place in the afternoon before it got dark. In the two photos above you can see the reconstructed Globe theatre, which continues to be popular with audiences. The modern Globe often uses Elizabethan costumes in its performances.

6.3 Education in the home, schools and universities

YOUR CHALLENGE

1. Use a chart such as the one on page 80 to collect evidence from boxes A–K on these pages which supports or challenges the following statement:

   The opportunities for better education increased during Elizabeth's reign.

2. Write a paragraph developing or correcting the statement above, using the evidence in your chart.

The number of children going to school increased during Elizabeth's reign. This tells us that it was a time of relative prosperity, when some people, at least, had enough money to pay for their children's education. In addition, learning was valued and individual aspirations were encouraged. However, for the majority of people, education was a luxury, especially when worried about starvation, taxation, war or disease. At times when the population was just trying to survive, most people did not send their sons to school regularly.

A. Most people were still too poor to send their children to school. By the end of Elizabeth's reign, 30 per cent of men and fewer than 10 per cent of women could read or write, although the majority of gentry and yeomen were literate.

B. Educational opportunities increased for all classes and ages, but it was mainly boys from well-off families who benefited the most. The upper classes increasingly saw a university education as necessary for a career at court.

C. A countryman, speaking in the early seventeenth century, said:

> This is all we go to school for: to read common prayers at church and set down common prices at markets, write a letter and make a bond, set down the day of our births, our marriage day, and make our wills when we are sick for the disposing of our goods when we are dead.

D.

▲ Discipline was harsh in many Elizabethan schools. Schoolmasters frequently used a birch rod to beat pupils who had not done their work or had broken a rule.

The background image shows a public school; these became really popular for the sons of the wealthy classes in Elizabeth's reign.

E. Education was mainly for well-off boys, but bright boys from the lower classes could go to grammar school, and even university if they had some financial support. Hardly any schooling was free – even schools for the lower classes often charged for coal, candles and educational materials. Even so, there is evidence of an expansion in education in Elizabeth's reign across all social classes. Approximately one-third of students who graduated from both Oxford and Cambridge came from the nobility and gentry, with the remainder coming from the lower classes: tradespeople, farmers and so on. Christopher Marlowe was the son of a cobbler, but he won a scholarship from his local school to go to Corpus Christi College, Cambridge.

F. Parish/Petty Schools were local schools where young children, from about ages four to seven, were taught to read and write as preparation for moving on to a grammar school. It was nearly always boys who attended, although there were a small number of girls from the upper classes. These schools could be attached to a grammar school, in which case the small boys would be taught by older pupils, or attached to a village church, or might even be in a local woman's house, the so-called dame schools.

G. Sons of gentry, merchants and yeomen would most likely go to a grammar school, from the ages of seven to fifteen, although a small number might attend one of the new public schools. During Elizabeth's reign, 72 new grammar schools were founded. Demand for places increased throughout the reign, from all social classes. The subjects taught were mainly Latin and Greek, as this study of the classics was thought to encourage intellectual, personal and spiritual growth. A typical day might include:
- Latin-to-English translations
- studying the writings of classical authors like Virgil and Cicero
- learning some Greek, and even Hebrew, to help with translations of the Scriptures
- arithmetic
- tests and exams.

H. The earliest independent or public schools were Winchester and Eton. These fee-paying boarding schools were set up for 'ruling-class boys'. All lessons were taught in Latin and the curriculum combined the methods of the grammar schools with an emphasis on the conduct, courtesy and etiquette (manners) necessary to produce gentlemen destined for careers at court.

I. At university, all degrees involved grammar, rhetoric (the art of developing arguments) and logic, with compulsory lectures in mathematics, music, theology, astronomy and geometry. Only after this could an undergraduate specialise. Most chose law, a traditional route into the professions for boys from non-noble classes. On completion of his education, a gentleman would be distinguishable from the lower classes because he could speak and write 'proper English' and had some knowledge of French and Latin. He would also have learned the correct social etiquette, particularly good table manners, and would know how to dance. The number of students entering the two universities of Oxford and Cambridge increased considerably under Elizabeth, as all classes realised the importance of higher education in getting to the top, or at least near it.

J. Sons of the nobility were first educated at home by a private tutor. At age fifteen, they would go to university, although some might first attend one of the new public schools. Daughters would also be educated at home. Most wealthy and titled women were able to read and write, and some, like Elizabeth herself, received an exceptional education at home, from their tutors.

K. Some of the lower classes were taught to read and write by their masters at their place of work, and in the case of servants and apprentices, this would probably be where they lived as well.

EDUCATION IN ELIZABETHAN ENGLAND?

1. What were the types of school available in Elizabethan England?
2. Describe two features of:
   a) grammar schools
   b) universities.
3. Who was taught at home?
4. Give three reasons why the Elizabethans valued education.

6.4 Reasons for the increase in poverty and vagabondage

YOUR CHALLENGE ?

Read pages 88–9 quickly, to get an overview of the content, then read them again and complete these tasks:

1. Use a chart such as the one on page 80 to collect evidence which supports or challenges the following statement:

   Fewer people were poor during Elizabeth's reign.

2. Write a paragraph developing or correcting the statement above, using the evidence in your chart.

3. Draw a spider diagram to summarise the causes of poverty.

4. Choose a range of years between 1558 and 1588 when poverty was particularly bad. Explain your choice.

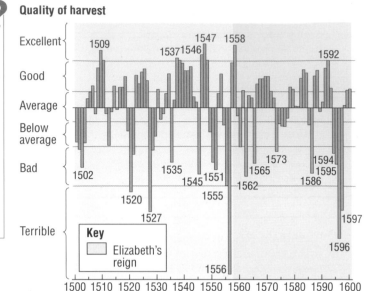

Quality of harvest

▲ Graph showing the quality of the harvests in England between 1500 and 1600. You saw part of this graph on page 28, showing the bad harvests before Elizabeth became Queen. Here we are using it to see the harvests during Elizabeth's reign. Remember that your course ends in 1588 so do not mention later events in your exam.

Harvests and changes in farming

Everyone depended on food grown by farmers, but farmers were at the mercy of the weather. The graph on the right shows exactly when there were good harvests and bad, and when people were in danger of starvation. You can see that the worst harvest of the century was in 1556, just before Elizabeth became Queen. During her reign, there were two really bad sequences of harvests, in the early 1570s and the mid-1590s. However, even one bad harvest caused food shortages and this meant that the price of bread and other foods went up. At these times, the poor suffered most because they struggled to afford higher bread prices.

Many farmers began to look for more profitable ways to earn their living, by switching to different methods of agriculture. One method was to enclose land with hedges and put sheep on it instead of growing crops. This saved the farmers money because they did not have to employ labourers to work the land. The village labourers who worked on this land lost their jobs and homes, and many moved to towns hoping to find work. Some landlords also increased the rent on the lands they rented out to farmers. This was called rack-renting. Many farmers could not afford to pay these higher rents, so they too moved to towns in search of work.

▼ Harvesting corn in the sixteenth century. By the reign of Elizabeth, about 85 per cent of the population still lived in the countryside, where the main occupation was farming.

Unemployment in industries

The only important industry in the sixteenth century was the cloth trade, where English woollen cloth was exported to Europe. This had provided work for many spinners and weavers. When the cloth trade collapsed in the 1550s (see top right graph), tens of thousands of people lost their jobs.

More and more people

The country's population had fallen by nearly half at the time of the Black Death in 1348–9. It remained low until the sixteenth century, when it began to increase. As you can see in the centre right graph, the rise in population became steeper in Elizabeth's reign. This rise in population meant that more jobs were needed, but as you have read above, there were fewer jobs in farming and the cloth industry. More and more people could not find work, so could not earn money.

Inflation – rising prices

Another problem creating poverty was inflation – prices were going up all across Europe. Look at the bottom right graph. The red line shows that wages began to rise in the 1550s and continued to rise until about 1570. After that, they increased very slowly. However prices, especially the price of food, rose much more steeply, especially after 1570. The result was that people, especially those on lower wages, struggled to afford even basic food. Prices might be going up, but their wages were not. Although historians do not all agree about the causes of inflation, most think that it was caused by an increase in demand for goods such as food, probably due to the growing population, and an inability to produce enough to meet this demand.

Henry VIII's debasement of the coinage in the 1540s, when he ordered all the coins to be melted down, also played a part in the rise in prices from the middle of the sixteenth century. These coins had contained precious metal like gold or silver, but when new coins were minted, they contained far less gold and silver. Henry made himself nearly a million pounds, but he had 'debased' the coinage. After this, people no longer trusted its value, so merchants and shopkeepers began to put up prices, so they felt they were getting the same value for what they sold.

The closure of the monasteries

Until the 1530s, the monasteries provided food and shelter for the homeless and unemployed. However, they were closed down by Henry VIII in the late 1530s. This Dissolution of the Monasteries meant there was less help for the poor, and many of them were left to wander the roads or drift to the towns in search of work.

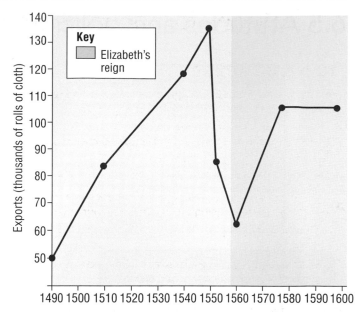

▲ Cloth exports from London in the sixteenth century. London was the country's biggest port.

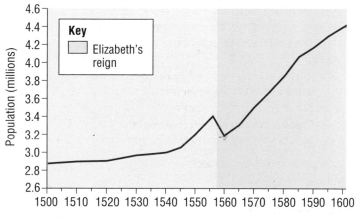

▲ The population of England and Wales, 1500–1600.

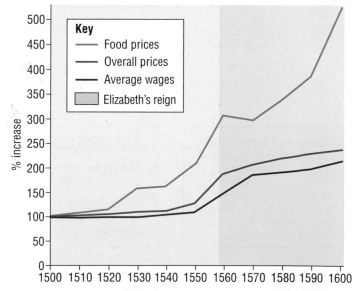

▲ Prices and wages in England, 1500–1600.

6.5 Attitudes and policies towards the poor

Most people believed that everyone should work hard to look after themselves and their families. They believed that beggars set a bad example. The Puritans felt very strongly about the importance of hard work. They believed that idleness was a sin because it displeased God, and that it was the Devil who made people idle, and so anyone who refused to work should be severely punished. Some of Elizabeth's Privy Councillors, Members of Parliament and JPs were Puritans.

In the sixteenth century, most people believed that everyone had a fixed place in society. Everyone was expected to obey their social superiors. As long as this happened, the wealth and power of the upper classes were protected. Large numbers of discontented beggars wandering around the countryside threatened the social order. They did not seem to know their place, and were not obeying their superiors. If this continued, tens of thousands of poor people might rebel and overthrow the ruling classes. This had nearly happened 200 years earlier, in the Peasants' Revolt of 1381.

Many people thought that there were huge numbers of vagabonds travelling around the country. Exaggerated writings by people like Thomas Harman helped to stir up a lot of unnecessary panic. Historians today think that there were nowhere near as many beggars as people at the time thought.

There were many outbreaks of plague and other infectious diseases in the sixteenth century. Many people died at an early age, but no one understood why. Most people believed that wandering groups of vagabonds spread deadly diseases.

Why were Elizabethans so worried about poverty?

Rich and powerful people were not only expected to control the lower classes; they also had a duty to help local people who had fallen on hard times. Many landowners took this seriously. They gave gifts of money and food to the poor. This was called Poor Relief. The monasteries helped them to care for the poor until Henry VIII closed them down. By Elizabeth's reign, many landowners could not cope with the growing numbers of poor people. They simply could not afford to help them all.

Beggars often turned to crime. Some of them robbed people in the streets and broke into their houses. There was no police force to catch criminals. The Justices of the Peace (JPs) were responsible for enforcing law and order in local areas. They wanted to do a good job for the Queen. They thought the beggars were a serious threat to their authority.

It is not easy to know what the poor themselves thought about poverty. They would certainly have seen beggars being whipped in the streets. Some poor people probably felt sorry for them and might have blamed rich people for being too greedy and cruel. Others would have been frightened by the beggars. The beggars might steal the few possessions they had. Perhaps they thought that beggars were giving all poor people a bad name. But this is largely guesswork – and guesswork is not good history.

Sixteenth-century governments were always worried about the danger of rebellions. They did not have a permanent army to deal with them. Rising numbers of poor people made the threat of rebellion even greater. Powerful people who opposed Elizabeth, such as discontented nobles or Mary, Queen of Scots, might try to win the support of the poor for a rebellion against Elizabeth's government.

Elizabeth's government
The government of Elizabeth I's reign was not what we would mean today by 'the government'. Elizabeth's government usually refers to her councillors, chosen by her and not elected.

YOUR CHALLENGE

1. Read the diagram above. Choose a heading for each paragraph to sum up the reasons why Elizabethans worried about poverty.

2. Use a chart such as the one on page 80 to collect evidence from pages 90–91 which supports or challenges the following statement:

   Elizabeth's government tried hard to help everyone who was poor.

3. Read page 91. Describe two features of the Acts passed by Elizabeth's government to tackle the problem of poverty.

4. How did the treatment of the poor change in Elizabeth's reign?

Vagabonds

Many Elizabethans were worried about the growing number of poor people, but particularly the vagabonds, wandering beggars who, it was said, were fit and strong, but deliberately avoided work. Stories were told of them travelling in groups, robbing and stealing as well as begging. Thomas Harman was so worried about vagabonds that he wrote a book so that people would not be taken in by them. Can you match Harman's categories of vagabond listed with the drawings below?

- Angler – used a long stick to steal clothes from washing lines
- Counterfeit crank – pretended to have a fit by swallowing soap and foaming at the mouth
- Clapper dudgeon – put arsenic on their skin to make it bleed and wrapped bandages around their arms and legs
- Doxy – carried a bag where she hid things she stole; often knitted while begging and wore a needle in her hat

A

B

C

D

Despite these fears, Elizabeth's government developed a varied approach to the poor:

- It accepted some responsibility for looking after the poor and thought that the rich should finance that help.
- It distinguished between the poor who wanted to work but could not (the 'deserving poor'), and those who were able-bodied but would not work (the 'idle poor', also known as 'sturdy beggars').

New laws – help and punishment

Elizabeth's government dealt differently with the deserving poor and the idle poor. Two Acts were passed by Parliament, telling towns how to deal with or help the poor. The main provisions of these Acts are set out below, and extracts A–C provide evidence of how individuals were treated.

Vagabonds Act, 1572

- Anyone found guilty of being a vagabond, over the age of 14, was to be whipped and burned through the right ear.
- For a second offence, vagabonds were to be sent to prison.
- Persistent offenders were to be executed.
- Children of convicted beggars were to be placed in domestic service.
- Local Justices of the Peace were ordered to keep a register of the poor in their parish, and to raise a poor rate to pay for food and shelter for the sick and elderly.

Act for Relief of the Poor, 1576

- Towns were required to find work for the able-bodied poor.
- Those refusing an offer of work were to be sent to a house of correction (prison).

Extract A from the records of law courts in Middlesex

1574: At Harrow Hill on 29 March John Allen, Elizabeth Turner, Humfrey Foxe, Henry Bower and Agnes Wort, being over 14 years old, and having no lawful means of livelihood, were vagrants, and had been vagrants in other parts of the country. Sentenced to be flogged severely and burnt on the right ear.

Extract B Norwich Census of the Poor, 1570

Peter Browne, a cobbler; 50 years old and hath little work. Agnes, his wife, of the age 52 years, that worketh not having been sick since Christmas. She spins wool. There are three daughters, one of 18 years, one of 13 years and the other of 14 years. They all spin when they can get work but now they are without work.

Extract C from Norwich city records

1570. A count shall be made of all the poor people who live in the city. Their need for alms shall be reviewed weekly.

1571. There shall be a workplace for men to grind malt and women to spin. The prisoners shall work for their meat and drink for at least 21 days: 15 hours a day in summer and 14 hours in winter. Those that refuse shall be whipped.

No person shall beg or they shall be whipped six times. No person shall feed or help any beggars at their door.

One officer shall go daily about the city, with a staff in his hand, and arrest any vagabonds.

There shall also be appointed select women to receive idle women or the poorest children into their houses to work or learn their letters.

Visible learning: revise and remember

1. Revising the 'Golden Age'

We introduced this section on pages 78–9, with the idea that Elizabeth's reign is often seen as a Golden Age. Here is a good way of linking your work in Chapter 6 to the arguments about whether Elizabeth's reign was a Golden Age.

1576 Act for Relief of the Poor

A Golden Age?

Evidence for   Evidence against

1. Create a set of cards which provide evidence about aspects of the topics in this chapter – leisure, education and poverty. On each card, put a heading and a short explanation of what this topic tells you about Elizabethan England.
2. Draw your own set of scales and place your cards on one side or the other – or create a third pile of cards which provide evidence which could support both interpretations, that it was and was not a Golden Age.

2. Improve your Word Wall

You have come across some new words in this chapter. Here are some of them:

- poor relief
- inflation
- debasement
- petty school
- public school
- vagabond
- idle poor.

1. Explain what each one means.
2. What other words from Chapter 6 should you add to your wall?

3. Test yourself!

1. List three reasons why the number of poor grew in Elizabeth's reign.	2. List three things taught at Elizabethan grammar schools.	3. Which rebellion took place in 1569?	4. How did Elizabeth's government tackle the problem of the poor in 1572 and 1576?	5. List three reasons explaining the popularity of the theatre in Elizabeth's reign.
6. Who was the leader of the Spanish Armada?	7. Give two examples of how vagabonds tried to make money.	8. Why did people like Christopher Marlowe's plays?	9. What was the name of the first theatre opened in London?	10. Name three people who plotted to restore Catholicism to England.

Practice questions

1. Describe two features of sports and pastimes for the wealthy.
2. Describe two features of sports and pastimes for ordinary people.
3. Explain why Elizabethans were worried about the 'idle poor' and vagabonds.
4. 'Poor harvests were the most important cause of poverty in Elizabeth's reign.' How far do you agree? Explain your answer.

7 Exploration, voyages of discovery, Raleigh and Virginia

European exploration of the wider world began in the late 1400s. One major aim was to search for the legendary north-west passage to the East: a route through to China, India and the silk and spice trades. Until Elizabeth's reign, England was very much the poor relation in exploration, which was dominated by Spain and Portugal. Sailors from these two **maritime empires** explored new continents, set up trade routes and conquered land and peoples, including the famous **Aztec** and **Inca** empires.

However, during Elizabeth's reign, English sailors and explorers challenged Spain in particular. Their voyages, particularly those of Francis Drake and Walter Raleigh, played a great part in creating Elizabeth's successful reputation. This chapter has two enquiries:

1. Why was there so much overseas exploration during Elizabeth's reign?
2. Were the voyages of Drake and Raleigh really so significant?

A modern reconstruction of the *Golden Hind*, built to ▶ commemorate the 400th anniversary of Francis Drake's circumnavigation of the world, 1577–80. About 60 men sailed with Drake in this 30-metre ship.

7.1 Your enquiry: why was there so much overseas exploration in Elizabeth's reign?

Creating and developing your hypothesis

In this enquiry, you will use a card sort to categorise and explain the reasons for overseas exploration taking place. The cards below show eight individual reasons for the voyages

Conflict with Spain	Expansion of trade	Desire to spread Protestantism	Duty to civilise other cultures
New technology in ships and sailing	Opportunity to make money	New learning and knowledge	Increased experience of sailors

1. We can organise these eight reasons into categories – reasons which have something important in common. What categories can you identify and how would you group the reasons into those categories?
2. Use the categories to draft a paragraph answering the question in the heading above. You should be well used to creating this kind of hypothesis paragraph by now.

Reasons for the growth of overseas exploration during Elizabeth's reign

ANALYSING THE REASONS FOR VOYAGES ?

1. Match the headings below to paragraphs 1–8 on pages 94–95.
   - ☐ Conflict with Spain
   - ☐ New technology in ships and sailing
   - ☐ Expansion of trade
   - ☐ Opportunity to make money
   - ☐ Desire to spread Protestantism
   - ☐ New learning and knowledge
   - ☐ Duty to civilise other cultures
   - ☐ Increased experience of sailors

2. The chart below shows three categories of reasons why voyages took place. Are they similar to the categories you came up with in activity 1 on page 93? Decide which headings and paragraphs should go in each column of the table. Some of the reasons may fit in more than one category.

Financial and military motives	To spread ideas and influence	Technical and educational reasons

3. Now write an answer to the following question:

Explain why English sailors went on so many voyages of discovery during Elizabeth's reign.

Use the Writing better history guidance on pages 114–123 to help you.

Visible learning

Effective reading

The most effective way to tackle each section is to read it at least twice! The first time, read it quickly to identify the main points. Do not worry too much about the detail. Then read it again, this time focusing on the detail that supports the main points

1. The growing wealth and power of Catholic Spain was based on the gold and silver mines of Spanish territories in the New World, mainly Mexico and Peru. The English desire to attack and plunder these territories increased as relations with Spain grew worse in the 1580s and English fears of a Catholic invasion grew. English explorers (pirates, in the eyes of the Spanish), like John Hawkins and Francis Drake, took no notice of trade restrictions on Spanish territories, especially once it was clear that Spain was no longer England's ally.

2. By the middle of the sixteenth century, developments in the design of ships and the navigational instruments they carried meant that sailors could make longer voyages than ever before. In 1569, the Flemish mapmaker, Gerardus Mercator, introduced sea charts showing the parallels of latitude and longitude. Elizabethan sailors could now use an astrolabe to determine their latitude by measuring the angle between the horizon and the North Star. By the Elizabethan period, astrolabes had become very sophisticated and consisted of a large brass ring fitted with a sighting rule. The use of the astrolabe, however, depended on visibility, so Elizabethan sailors tended to rely more on the magnetic compass. Again, these were not new, and it had long been realised that the magnetic north which the compass needle pointed to was not true north. The Elizabethan mathematician and astronomer, Sir John Dee, developed 'an instrument magneticall for the finding of the variation of the compasse', which now enabled sailors to take readings from both compasses, calculate the variation according to the position of the ship and determine true north.

English sailors also benefited from the new technology in shipbuilding developed by the Portuguese earlier in the century to produce the massive galleon and the more compact caravel. These two new designs enabled expeditions to be planned across the Atlantic with stronger and faster ships, with an increased carrying capacity. Ships were now fitted with triangular sails, which could easily be turned to catch the strong winds of the open seas, and with sophisticated artillery, including the more rapid-firing guns (see page 74). Explorers like Drake could also benefit from the knowledge brought back by earlier navigators. Drake took with him charts and books of navigation written by Portuguese sailors.

3. Before the 1550s, nearly all English trade was concentrated on exporting woollen cloth to Europe; this had accounted for 75 per cent of all exports and brought in annual customs duties of between £35,000 and £50,000. Once this trade collapsed, English merchants needed to find new markets to sell their goods. This motivated journeys overland, as well as overseas, with some Elizabethan explorers establishing trade agreements with countries as far away as Russia and India. The most lucrative form of trade, however, was the illegal trade of selling items, including slaves, to the Spanish colonists in the New World.

4. Many of the English upper classes, including the Queen, were prepared to put up the money for overseas voyages as a way of making a quick profit. Attacks on Spanish cargo ships, like the *Cacafuego* (see page 100), carrying gold and silver to Europe, resulted in a fast and big profit for any investors, although they were technically acts of piracy. At a lower level, signing on as a sailor ensured a regular wage and offered a way out of the poverty experienced by some of the labouring classes, especially those living near ports.

5. Converting heathen lands to Christianity had long been the motive behind many of the earlier Spanish expeditions. Individual popes had blessed those Jesuit priests who undertook terrifying journeys as missionaries in far-off lands. Elizabethan explorers were no different, although their aim was to spread Protestantism, and in their case, this was to be largely achieved by holding back the continuing expansion of their Catholic enemies.

6. The increase in learning due to the ideas of the Renaissance encouraged a thirst for knowledge and adventure that drove curious Elizabethans to explore beyond the limits of their own known world. Many believed there was a route westwards across the Atlantic that would lead directly to the riches of the East, places like China and India. The invention of the printing press enabled books to reach a wider audience, such as Richard Hakluyt's *The Principal Navigations, Voyages and Discoveries of the English Nation*, which urged sailors to go on longer voyages. Some gentlemen-at-arms, like Francis Petty who sailed with Drake, kept logs of their voyages; and, of course, men like Drake and Raleigh acted as role models for others who looked to expand their horizons.

7. The confident Elizabethans felt it was their duty to spread the advantages of their age and country to other lands. Raleigh named the first American colony 'Virginia', in honour of the Virgin Queen. Elizabethan explorers believed the Native Americans could only benefit from their civilising influence, as these extracts from Richard Hakluyt show:

All savages, so soon as they begin to taste of civilisation, will take marvellous delight in any garment – as a shirt, a gown a cap or suchlike.

But that is not all the benefit which they shall receive; they shall be reduced from unseemly customs to honest manners, from disordered riotous routs [...] to a well governed commonwealth.

8. English seamen were well trained, as most had grown up in seafaring communities on the coast and had worked as merchant seamen. They were often used to smuggling or even piracy. Experienced captains such as Drake and Hawkins were not just successful in leading overseas voyages, they also inspired great loyalty and affection from their crews, who were prepared to follow them anywhere.

7.2 Your enquiry: were the voyages of Drake and Raleigh really so significant?

Sir Hugh Willoughby and Richard Chancellor, 1553
Willoughby and Chancellor thought that they could reach China by sailing around the north of Asia. They set sail in 1553. Willoughby was killed when his ship was trapped in ice north of Norway. Chancellor reached Muscovy (Moscow in modern Russia). Soon afterwards, the Muscovy Company was formed to trade with Russia.

John Hawkins, 1562–68
Hawkins made three voyages during the 1560s. He sailed to the west coast of Africa and captured Africans. Then he sailed to the West Indies and Central America to sell the people he had captured as slaves to Spanish settlers. In 1567, during his third voyage, the Spanish attacked his fleet. Hawkins lost four ships and over 200 men. After this, Hawkins worked in England designing and building ships for the navy.

John Cabot, 1497
Cabot was an Italian sailor. He thought he could reach India by sailing north of America. Henry VII agreed to fund his voyage. Cabot set sail in 1497. He reached Newfoundland, off the coast of modern Canada. There were good fishing grounds there but no gold, silk or spices. He went on a second voyage in 1498, but never returned.

Sir Walter Raleigh, 1595
In 1595 Raleigh set sail for South America. He was hoping to find El Dorado, a legendary city full of gold. He reached Guiana and sailed up the River Orinoco, but did not find the city, nor any gold.

John Davis, 1585–87
Davis made three voyages to North America, in search of a route to China. He reached Baffin Island, but was stopped from getting further by the cold and ice.

BAFFIN ISLAND

ENGLAND

NEWFOUNDLAND

NORTH AMERICA

VIRGINIA

Atlantic Ocean

GUIANA

Pacific Ocean

SOUTH AMERICA

Key

- Spanish empire
- Portuguese empire
- New trading areas established during Elizabeth's reign

EARLY TUDOR EXPLORERS
- John Cabot
- Willoughby and Chancellor

ELIZABETHAN EXPLORERS
- John Hawkins
- Martin Frobisher
- Francis Drake
- Humphrey Gilbert
- Sir Walter Raleigh
- John Davis
- Sir Walter Raleigh

English voyages of exploration, 1558–88

These two pages summarise the major voyages of exploration during Elizabeth's reign.
Your detailed enquiry begins on page 98.

Martin Frobisher, 1576
Frobisher believed that it was possible to reach China by sailing around North America. In 1576, he reached Baffin Island in the Arctic. He found a black rock, which he hoped would contain gold – but he was wrong. He made two more voyages but each time was forced back by the cold and ice.

Francis Drake, 1577–80
In 1577 Francis Drake set sail to attack Spanish settlements in Central America. He sailed around South America and attacked Spanish towns in Mexico, capturing gold, silver and jewels. He returned to England by sailing across the Pacific and Indian Oceans and then up the west coast of Africa. Drake became the first Englishman to sail around the world. He made a large profit from the voyage.

Moscow

A S I A

CHINA

Sir Humphrey Gilbert, 1583
Sir Humphrey Gilbert wanted to establish an English settlement in North America. He also believed that there was a route to China around North America. He set sail in 1583 and reached Newfoundland. He explored the coast of North America but his ship was hit by storms. He never returned.

INDIA

THE EAST INDIES OR 'SPICE ISLANDS'

AFRICA

Indian Ocean

AUSTRALIA

Pacific Ocean

Sir Walter Raleigh, 1585-87
Sir Walter Raleigh was a famous sailor and courtier. He wanted to establish an English COLONY in North America. He called it Virginia, in honour of Elizabeth, the Virgin Queen. He organised two expeditions to take settlers to the colony. The first settlers came home after one year. The second group were never seen again.

ELIZABETHAN VOYAGES – AN OUTLINE ❓

1 Which types of voyage were the most successful, and why?

2 Which types of voyage were unsuccessful? What reasons can you suggest for their failure?

3 What do you think was the main achievement of the voyages made in Elizabeth's reign? Explain the reasons for your answer.

WHAT MADE VOYAGES SIGNIFICANT?

Drake and Raleigh come at the top of any list of names explaining why Elizabeth's reign is often called a Golden Age. However, just as with our investigation of the reputation of the Queen herself, we need to dig a little deeper and find out whether their voyages were really significant rather than just famous.

To make a judgement, you need to find out about the voyages themselves, but also about what they achieved – if anything. You will also need to make some comparison between the two men – were the voyages of one more significant than those of the other? Here are the tasks that will help you with this enquiry.

1. Decide on your criteria for significance – what would make a voyage of exploration significant? The table below shows four criteria. Decide if you think these are all the criteria needed or whether others should be added. For example, should the long-term effects of these voyages be included?

2. Draw your own copy of this table, with your criteria at the top. Read the pages shown in the table and then:
   a) put a small tick in the columns, identifying which criteria each voyage meets
   b) add a short description, noting how important the voyage was. For example, did Drake's voyage of circumnavigation have a 'major' impact on England's status or a 'limited' impact? Did Raleigh's 1585 voyage bring home 'considerable' riches or 'some' riches?
   c) Make separate notes justifying your descriptions of the effects of each voyage.

	Discovered new lands/sea routes	Established new trading opportunities	Brought home riches	Increased England's status and power
Drake's voyage				
1577–80 Circumnavigation of the world (pages 98–101)				
Raleigh's voyages				
1585 Established an English colony in North America (page 103)				
1587 Second expedition to establish a colony in Virginia (page 104)				

Drake's circumnavigation of the world, 1577–80

Drake's aims

Drake's voyages of 1568 and 1572 (described on pages 99–101) left him with a hatred of Catholic Spain and a desire to inflict further damage on its empire. The aims of this voyage were:

- revenge for the Spanish attack on Hawkins's fleet in 1568 (see page 4). He planned to attack Spanish settlements in Central America from the direction of the Pacific Ocean, where defences were weaker.
- to capture Spanish gold, silver and other treasure, both to make money for himself and to reward courtiers who had invested in his expedition. Drake's investors included the Queen, but because she was worried that Drake's activities would cause trouble with Spain, her support was kept quiet.
- Drake was a Puritan, so wanted to weaken the greatest Catholic power in Europe. A weaker Spain would also make England more secure from attack.
- Drake hoped to find new lands to claim for the Queen. This would make England more powerful.
- Drake wanted to establish new and better trade routes, and find new markets where English merchants could sell their goods overseas. Many of his investors were merchants.

Drake's ships

Drake's ship was the 80-ton *Pelican*, later renamed the *Golden Hind* (see photo on page 93). He sailed with four other ships. The *Elizabeth* was a similar size and was captained by John Winter. The three smaller ships were:

- the *Marigold*, a **bark** of 30 tons captained by John Thomas
- the *Swan*, a **flyboat** of 50 tons captained by John Chester
- the *Christopher*, a **pinnace** of 15 tons captained by Thomas Moore.

In total, there was a crew of 164 sailors. The initial omens were not good. After setting sail from Plymouth on 15 November, the five ships encountered such severe storms that they returned to Plymouth for repairs three days later.

▲ Differences in the size of Drake's *Golden Hind* and the modern-day container ships which make the same trip across the Atlantic.

Stage 1: sailing to Brazil, December 1577–April 1578

The fleet set sail from Plymouth again in December, and sailed south down the west coast of Africa to the Cape Verde Islands. Here, they captured a Portuguese ship and its cargo of wine. They took it with them across the Atlantic Ocean. As they neared the Equator and the coast of Brazil, quarrels began to break out among the crew. One of them, John Cooke, who sailed on the *Elizabeth*, wrote:

> We met with adverse winds, unwelcome storms and less welcome calms. Being in the burning zone, we felt the effects of sultry heat.

DRAKE'S VOYAGE: STAGE 1　?

1. Summarise each of Drake's aims in one or two words.
2. After the first five months at sea, had Drake achieved any of his aims?
3. What problems had the expedition met with?
4. What effect would these problems have on the sailors and on the voyage's chances of success?

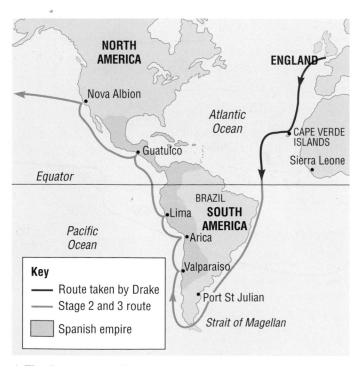

▲ The first stage of Drake's voyage.

▲ Engraving of Francis Drake at the River Plate, 11 December 1578, by Johannes Baptista in 1610. This area was visited by Drake's fleet in the first half of 1578, in the early stages of his circumnavigation.

Stage 2: sailing from Brazil to Guatulco, April 1578–April 1579

The fleet sailed down the coast of Brazil, reaching Port St Julian on 20 June 1578. When some of the crew went ashore to trade, they were involved in a fight with local people and two sailors were killed. Tensions among the crew grew worse until Drake was forced to charge his friend, Sir Thomas Doughty, for reasons that are still unclear to us, with **mutiny**, and order his execution. Drake then put all his men and stores onto his three best ships, burning the others.

The reduced fleet continued down the east coast of South America, entering the dangerous Strait of Magellan at the bottom of the continent, on 21 August. It was here that Drake's voyage added considerably to the knowledge of world geography at that time. He discovered that Tierra del Fuego, the land seen to the south of the Magellan Strait, was not a large southern continent, as had been supposed, but a group of islands. This opened up the possibility of sailing to the Cape of Good Hope, the southern tip of the African continent, by going south of Tierra del Fuego.

In September, Drake's remaining three ships reached the Pacific Ocean and made their way up the west coast of South America. They were hit by stormy weather which lasted for about a month. The *Marigold* sank and the *Elizabeth* got lost, but eventually managed to find her way back to England. The loss of the *Elizabeth* meant that Drake was left with just one ship, which was running low on food and water. However, when he landed on the island of Mocha to take on water, he was attacked by its inhabitants. Drake was wounded by arrows to the face and head.

The last part of this stage, however, resulted in far more success. After they recovered from their wounds, Drake and the crew attacked Spanish settlements along the coast of Peru. At Valparaiso, they captured gold, coins and supplies of wine; at Arica, they seized 57 ingots (bars) of silver; and at the port of Lima, they attacked twelve ships loaded with silk and Spanish coins. Then Drake heard that the *Cacafeugo*, a Spanish treasure ship, had recently left port. He gave chase and captured its cargo, containing, according to John Drake:

> A certain quantity of jewels and precious stones, thirteen chests of coins, 80 pounds weight of gold, 26 tons of silver and two very fair gilt drinking bowls.

Finally, Drake and his crew attacked Guatulco, seizing yet more silver, gold and jewels.

DRAKE'S VOYAGE: STAGE 2

1. What were the high and low points of this second stage of Drake's circumnavigation?
2. Did Drake achieve any of his aims during these twelve months?
3. Could any of these achievements be said to be significant, and, if so, why?

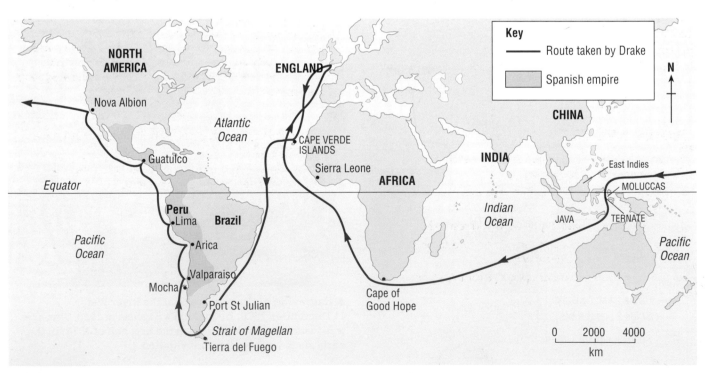

▲ Drake's circumnavigation of the world.

Stage 3: sailing from South America to Plymouth, April 1579–September 1580

At Guatulco, Drake had to decide on his route to return to England. If he turned round and retraced his steps, he would face certain attacks from Spanish ships who would be expecting him. He would also have to go back through the treacherous Magellan Strait. Drake showed his daring and desire to learn more by deciding to find a route back to England around North America.

By now, Drake had only one ship and about 55 men. Even so, he sailed up the coast of North America to a latitude no English explorer had ever reached before.

He landed in California and claimed it for Queen Elizabeth, naming it Nova Albion (New England). This claim to California was the basis of future plans to establish colonies of English settlers in America. The native peoples of California thought Drake was a god and gave him presents of feathers and tobacco.

From California, Drake sailed west across the Pacific Ocean and, after two months, reached the Molucca Islands, where locals gave him food and water. He then sailed on to Ternate, famous for its spices. Drake made a trade treaty with the king of the island, which allowed English merchants to trade in spices. He loaded up the *Golden Hind* with tons of cloves, ginger and pepper, although most had to be thrown overboard in January in order to lighten the ship's load when it ran aground on dangerous rocks. Drake's route through the East Indies, or Spice Islands, then followed the uncharted southern coast of Java. Drake discovered that Java was an island and not connected to a southern continent, as earlier Dutch explorers had believed. Then Drake sailed across the Indian Ocean, past the Cape of Good Hope and up the coast of West Africa. His first question when he reached land in Plymouth on 26 September 1580, was whether the Queen was still alive.

▲ Francis Drake was treated as a national hero, as this portrait shows. The Queen knighted him aboard the *Golden Hind*. He had brought back gold, silver and jewels worth about £140,000 (about £200 million pounds today). The Queen's share enabled her to pay off the national debt. He had successfully challenged the invincibility of the Spanish Empire, which encouraged others to do the same; he had claimed new lands for England, made valuable trading contacts with the Spice Islands and increased knowledge of the known world.

DRAKE'S VOYAGE: STAGE 3 ?

1. What have you learned about Drake's skills as a commander and as a sailor?
2. How successful do you think Drake was in achieving his aims?
3. Did the voyage have any unexpected results?
4. Could any of these achievements be said to be 'significant'? If so, explain why.
5. Complete your table from page 98 for this voyage.

1 Why does this portrait show Drake with both a helmet and a globe?
2 Why would the Queen in particular have been delighted with Drake's return home?

Were the voyages of Sir Walter Raleigh really significant?

Walter Raleigh was born to a gentry family in the West Country and educated locally. In the 1570s, he served in the French Religious Wars as a volunteer in the French Protestant army, and later commanded a company sent to put down rebellion in Ireland. At court, his 'dashing and flamboyant nature' caught Elizabeth's attention and he became a close favourite. In 1578, he was given command of his first ship, the *Falcon*, and sailed with his half-brother, the explorer Sir Humphrey Gilbert, to North America to establish an English settlement there. Despite reaching the coast of Nova Scotia, they were unable to secure a suitable location and Gilbert drowned when his ship sank.

Over the next ten years, Raleigh continued to be the Queen's favourite at court. Elizabeth knighted him, made him Captain of the Queen's Bodyguard and Vice-Admiral of Devon and Cornwall. He was also given considerable lands in England and Ireland. In 1584, he persuaded Elizabeth to agree to an expedition to explore the coast of North America, which he would name Virginia, in her honour. She gave Raleigh, in effect, exclusive rights to possess and exploit all the resources of the area, including minerals – except where there were other Europeans already established. You can see a scroll opposite that shows the advantages for Elizabeth and England of having colonies in North America.

Advantages of establishing a colony in North America:

To have a base for attacking Spanish interests in the area.

To launch raids on the Spanish West Indies and annual treasure fleets.

To prevent the Spanish and the French from settling there.

To provide the prospect of a better life for the growing number of poor in England.

To gain access to rich local resources, including minerals.

To add to the territories under the English crown and so increase its prestige.

WHAT DID RALEIGH ACTUALLY DO?

Sir Walter Raleigh was responsible for planning, organising and financing the two voyages that sailed in his name in 1585 and 1587 to establish English colonies in America. However, it is important to remember that Raleigh himself did not sail with them. Despite this, they are referred to as his voyages and he is given the credit for founding Virginia. The voyages which Raleigh led himself came after 1588, towards the end of Elizabeth's reign.

▲ Sir Walter Raleigh, 1552–1618. The portrait is thought to have been painted in 1588, by an artist known simply as 'H'.

The 1585 voyage

In April 1584, Raleigh dispatched two small ships on a reconnaissance expedition to the area off modern-day North Carolina. When they returned, the commanders gave enthusiastic reports of a fertile land, full of animals that could be hunted for food, and with civilised Native Americans. Raleigh began to organise his first expedition. As the Queen would not allow her favourite to leave court, in 1585, 108 male settlers, under the command of Ralph Lane, sailed to America with Sir Richard Grenville.

The settlement got off to an unfortunate start when Grenville's ship hit rocks as it came into land. The resulting seawater in the hold damaged supplies and seed crops. Lane began the construction of a fort and settlement on Roanoke Island, and after a couple of months, Grenville returned to England to get more settlers and supplies, leaving the **garrison** of 108 men. Relations with the local Native American population were not hostile at first, but some tribes started to get angry that the colonists were taking up good land and resources. Lane was forced to abandon Roanoke Island in June 1586, owing to hostilities between the English and the local Secotans on whom Lane's men depended for food. When Francis Drake arrived at the colony on his way home from the West Indies in the same month, starving colonists climbed aboard his ships to go back to England.

On his return to Court, Ralph Lane enthused about the virtues of Chesapeake Bay as the best place for a settlement, because it would enable searches for the gold mines which the Native Americans had told him about and a passage for boats through to the east. Raleigh, who by now had been knighted by the Queen and made 'Lord and Governor of Virginia', began to sponsor another expedition.

RALEIGH'S 1585 VOYAGE ?

1. Why do you think the Queen gave permission for Raleigh to establish a colony in North America?

2. Describe two features of the first settlement.

3. What problems did this settlement face? Was anyone to blame for these? If so, explain why.

4. Did this first expedition achieve anything?

5. Could it be said to be 'significant' in any way?

▲ A 1590 engraving of the arrival of the English in Virginia, by Theodor de Bry. De Bry was a Belgian engraver, editor and publisher, who produced many engravings about the arrival of the early Europeans in the Americas. This one was based on Thomas Hariot's book about the 1585 expedition, but de Bry's work was not particularly reliable. He never visited the New World and his Native Americans are said to look more like eastern Europeans. Nevertheless, his books, illustrations and engravings influenced European perceptions of the New World.

The 1587 voyage

Raleigh was determined to learn from the information brought back from the first colony. His second expedition took settler families rather than soldiers, headed further north to Chesapeake Bay, which was a better harbour. This expedition, led by John White, who had been on the two previous voyages, sailed in 1587. However, it was forced to land again in North Carolina when the master pilot, Simon Fernandes, who was worried about hurricanes, put the settlers off at Roanoke Island and refused to take them any further.

They established a second colony there, but it was too late to plant seeds and, again, relations with the local Native Americans were poor. White decided to return to England to bring back more supplies, but by then, all ships were needed for defence against the Armada. He was unable to return to Roanoke until 1590, when he found that the settlers he had left behind had disappeared, leaving only a message saying 'CRO'. It was widely believed that this meant the colonists had moved to the nearby island of Croatoan, but continued bad weather meant White could not reach them, and in the end he returned to England.

The colonists were never seen again and this has since become known as the 'Lost Colony'. Most historians think that the lost colonists encountered either disease or violence, split up into smaller groups and spread out among Native American villages. However, in 2013, archaeologists discovered a small Native American town to the west of Roanoke. Using modern equipment, they found evidence of wooden structures about a metre below the surface. Work is continuing to try to determine if this is the lost colony of Roanoke.

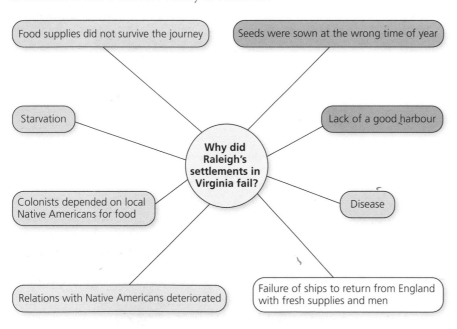

- Food supplies did not survive the journey
- Seeds were sown at the wrong time of year
- Starvation
- Lack of a good harbour
- **Why did Raleigh's settlements in Virginia fail?**
- Colonists depended on local Native Americans for food
- Disease
- Relations with Native Americans deteriorated
- Failure of ships to return from England with fresh supplies and men

▲ One of John White's watercolours, showing an Native American 'werowance', or chief.

THE 1587 VOYAGE?

1 How did Raleigh try to improve upon his first expedition, and why did this not work?

2 Why do we know more about the first expedition than the second?

3 Can any achievements of the 1587 voyage be described as significant? Give reasons for your answer.

4 Complete your table from page 98 for this Raleigh voyage.

Raleigh's expeditions, although perhaps not seen as a success at the time, had:

- laid the foundations for the eventual colonisation of America by the English in the next century
- returned a profit, due to captured Spanish ships
- excited merchants with examples of goods to trade, including the potato
- increased knowledge of the continent through:
  - increased navigational knowledge
  - the books of Thomas Hariot, Raleigh's assistant, who went on the 1585 voyage to Roanoke, which described the plants, animals and minerals of the area in great detail
  - the paintings of John White who was hired by Raleigh to record the expedition. His illustrations provide a remarkable array of evidence of the people and places White and his colleagues encountered.

7.3 Completing your enquiry

You should now have completed your Knowledge Organiser from page 98, assessing the significance of Drake's and Raleigh's voyages by measuring them against your criteria. It is now time to answer your enquiry question, but we have changed the style a little so that it fits the style of question you will answer in your examination:

'The most important consequence of the voyages of Drake and Raleigh was the wealth they brought back to England.' Do you agree? Explain your answer.

Use your Knowledge Organiser and the evidence you have collected.

1   Decide whether you agree or disagree with the statement in the question and then write a short paragraph directly answering the question.

2   Create an essay plan using your criteria, discussing one criterion in each paragraph and adding evidence from the voyages to support your judgements.

Use the writing guidance on pages 120–121 on answering this kind of question to help you.

Remember to use **connectives** to tie in the factors to the question.

Communicating your answer

Remember to use connective phrases; this is important when you have a question centred on a single word. You should try to avoid repeating, 'this was significant because …' all the time, so your answer does not read too much like a shopping list. Other connectives you might be able to use include: '… had an effect on', 'led to …', 'this caused …', '… made people think because …', '… changed the nature of …'.

And keep your Word Wall up to date!

Here are some of the words or phrases from this chapter that you will find useful.

Practice questions

1. Describe two features of the attempts to colonise Virginia in the 1580s.
2. Describe two features of Drake's circumnavigation of the world.
3. Explain why men such as Francis Drake went on voyages of exploration.
4. 'Relations with the Native Americans were the main reason for the failure of the Virginia colonies.' How far do you agree? Explain your answer.
5. 'The success of Drake's circumnavigation was due solely to his skills as a sailor.' How far do you agree? Explain your answer.
6. 'Events in the New World were the main reason for the breakdown of relations with Spain.' How far do you agree? Explain your answer. (Look back at Chapter 5 to refresh your memory.)

trade routes   colonies   plunder   New World   navigators   investors

heathen   logs   merchant   seafaring   settlement   goods   flyboat

pinnace   bark   latitude   uncharted   explored   expansion   lucrative

technology   technically   motive   largely   continuing   significant   founding

financing   establish   illegal   treacherous   invincibility

Elizabethan society in the age of exploration, 1558–88: review

Elizabethan society in the age of exploration is difficult to summarise. For everyone who did well and would have supported the rule of Elizabeth – Protestants, gentry, yeoman farmers, courtiers and playwrights – there was an opposite – Catholics, traditional nobles, the poor – who saw their quality of life deteriorating. Nevertheless, today the image remains of a dynamic period of history, with a Queen who showed some awareness of the plight of her people and took some responsibility for it.

In the sixteenth century, people expected that their monarch would protect them from invasions and crime, but there was no welfare state providing benefits or healthcare for them to fall back on in times of hardship. However, Elizabeth and her government took the first steps towards the state providing the poor and unemployed with food, shelter and even work. In education, Elizabethan England benefited from the ideas of the Renaissance and the invention of the printing press. Learning became more valued. In addition, voyages to other parts of the world increased people's knowledge of the world as a whole.

The influence of the Queen on the cultural developments of her reign was huge. She not only enjoyed the arts, music, dancing and drama, but she also sponsored actors and artists. The result of this was that the Queen herself became the subject of many paintings, plays and poems, as this extract from Edmund Spenser's *The Faerie Queen* (1589) shows:

> O goddess heavenly bright,
>
> Mirror of grace and majesty divine,
>
> Great lady of the greatest isle, whose light
>
> Like Phoebus' lamp (the sun) throughout the world does shine.

Social life at court revolved around masques, musical evenings and plays, and these cultural activities created a bond between the Queen and her courtiers. The upper classes recreated these pastimes and interests in their own homes.

To some extent, popular culture copied elite culture. The lower classes, too, bought art and sang songs – only these would be cheaper miniatures of the Queen and bawdy ballads, instead of madrigals. Some aspects of popular culture were 'stage-managed' by Elizabeth's government because they saw an opportunity to promote the image of a successful queen ruling over a loyal and happy people. The spider diagram below summarises the Queen's influence on leisure activities.

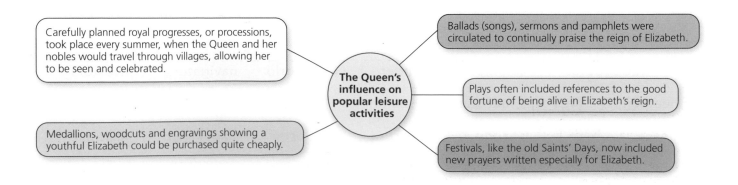

Carefully planned royal progresses, or processions, took place every summer, when the Queen and her nobles would travel through villages, allowing her to be seen and celebrated.

Ballads (songs), sermons and pamphlets were circulated to continually praise the reign of Elizabeth.

The Queen's influence on popular leisure activities

Plays often included references to the good fortune of being alive in Elizabeth's reign.

Medallions, woodcuts and engravings showing a youthful Elizabeth could be purchased quite cheaply.

Festivals, like the old Saints' Days, now included new prayers written especially for Elizabeth.

Visible learning: revise and remember

1. The scales of reputation!

At the end of Key Topic 2, you reviewed Elizabeth's reputation in the light of the contents of Chapters 4 and 5. It is time to repeat that task, but this time it is harder and even better for revision.

Elizabeth deserves a successful reputation

Elizabeth does NOT deserve a successful reputation

1. Make a set of cards listing the events and actions from Chapters 6 and 7 that you would place on the scales.
2. Decide which cards you would put on each side.
3. Write a short answer to the following question: 'The developments in Elizabethan society show that Elizabeth's successful reputation was fully justified.' How far do you agree? Explain your answer.

2. Alternative stories

Revise the stories of the events you have studied about Elizabethan society in Chapters 6 and 7 by describing events from the perspective of one individual. This helps you to recap the story, but also helps you realise that people had different attitudes to the events that took place. Work in groups of two or three and choose one of the individuals below. Write a short account of these years, giving your reactions to the major events.

- A boy attending grammar school
- An actor
- A nobleman or his wife
- A farmworker in danger of losing his job
- A beggar who cannot find work
- Francis Drake
- Walter Raleigh
- John White

3. Test yourself!

The more you think about what you have learned, and **especially what you are not sure about**, the more chance you have of succeeding in your exam. So answer these questions and do not be surprised if you have seen some of them before.

1. When did Francis Drake sail around the world?	2. What did Puritans dislike about Elizabeth's Church of England?	3. Give three reasons to explain why there were more poor people in Elizabeth's reign.	4. How did houses change in Elizabeth's reign?	5. Give three reasons why Elizabethans went on voyages overseas.
6. Why did the Queen keep quiet about supporting these voyages?	7. Name two members of Elizabeth's first Privy Council.	8. Give three reasons why all classes enjoyed going to the theatre.	9. What new geographical knowledge did Drake discover?	10. What were the main causes of the Revolt of the Northern Earls?
11. Describe two features of Elizabeth's Religious Settlement of 1559.	12. Give three reasons why the settlers from the first Virginia colony decided to return home with Drake.	13. Why did Elizabeth execute Mary, Queen of Scots?	14. Why did Raleigh organise a second colony on Virginia when the first one had failed?	15. Give three reasons why England and Spain went to war in 1585.

4. Set questions yourself!

Work in a group of three. Each of you should set four revision questions on Key Topic 3. Use the style of questions on page 8. Then ask each other the questions – and make sure you know the answers to the questions you have set!

The year 1588 was a significant one, and not just because it is the end of your GCSE course. The defeat of the Spanish Armada was a high point in Elizabeth's reign. It raised the status of the Queen and the country throughout Western Europe. The Queen, however, was now aged 55, an old woman by the standards of the day. Elizabeth was to reign for another fifteen years, but as she, her ministers and policies grew increasingly old and out of touch, we need to ask the question: how did the issues of these last fifteen years affect her reputation?

8.1 The last years 1588–1603

THE LAST YEARS, 1588–1603 ?

Read through the four problems in the newspaper extracts on page 109 and then answer the following questions:

1. Which of the issues between 1558 and 1603 enhanced Elizabeth's reputation, and which issues damaged it?

2. How would you describe the last fifteen years of Elizabeth's reign? Which of the following descriptions best fits your view?
   ☐ 'A glorious sunset'
   ☐ 'Her best days had gone'
   ☐ 'An unsuccessful end to an over-rated reign'.

▶ This portrait, showing Elizabeth as an old woman, was painted in the 1620s, after she was dead. Is this what Elizabeth really looked like towards the end of her reign? Her English subjects would never have seen an image like this while Elizabeth was alive. Her government continued to portray the Queen as a powerful and dynamic ruler loved by her people.

Harvests got worse

By 1603, England's population had increased to four million. Some people had grown very prosperous, but many faced real hardship. Four terrible harvests (1594–7) meant big increases in the price of food, and as a result, there were local food riots. Hunger, combined with the high taxes and outbreaks of plague, led to an increase in both poverty and crime at the end of the 1590s. The government responded by passing the Elizabethan Poor Law of 1601, a ground-breaking achievement, with the state taking full responsibility for helping the deserving poor for the first time. It remained in force for the next 300 years.

War Continued

The defeat of the Armada did not end the war with Spain. Elizabeth had to commit to sending military force to help the Netherlands and France in their struggles against Spain. At the same time, rebellion broke out in Ireland. England's resources were really stretched and Elizabeth struggled to keep English forces fighting in so many areas. Success did not come until the very end of the reign.

Taxes Increased

The cost of the war with Spain meant people had to pay higher taxes. When these were not enough, Elizabeth introduced even more unpopular ways of raising money, like monopolies.

Earl of Essex rebelled – February 1601

By 1601, Elizabeth's leading advisers had all died, and the younger men she replaced them with were ambitious and impatient for power. One of these, Robert Devereux, the Earl of Essex, enjoyed a close, some would say flirtatious, relationship with the Queen. However, when she sent him to Ireland to lead her forces to put down the rebellion, things went very wrong. Essex's campaign was a complete disaster and he was put under house arrest for disobeying orders and deserting his post. When his monopoly on sweet wines was withdrawn, a now destitute Essex led an uprising of 300 of his followers into London. Essex was overpowered and then found guilty of treason, and executed on the orders of a tearful Queen.

How did Elizabethan England end?

By December 1602, Elizabeth seemed to be very frail, and her health continued to deteriorate, although her Council kept this secret so as not to spoil her reputation. The Queen lost her appetite and found it hard to sleep or speak. She still refused to name her successor. Elizabeth I died in her sleep on 24 March 1603. She was 69 years old and had been Queen of England for 44 years. After a **state funeral**, she was buried at Westminster Abbey four days later. As soon as she died, a messenger rode north to Edinburgh to inform the Queen's nearest relative, King James VI of Scotland – the son of Mary, Queen of Scots – that he was now King of England, too. The Tudor dynasty had reached its end.

8.2 Does Elizabeth deserve her successful reputation?

In the review at the end of Key Topic 1, on page 42, we introduced the controversy that surrounds Elizabeth's reputation. One of the reasons historians cannot agree is because Elizabeth and her government were so good at presenting the reign in a positive light that it is difficult to know what it was really like. It is hard to find out what people at the time thought because nobody was willing to criticise the Queen.

Now that you have completed your study of Elizabethan England, you are in a better position to decide whether you think the popular view of Elizabeth as Gloriana, ruling over a Golden Age in English history, is the one you most agree with. To help you reach your conclusion, here are some more historians' verdicts about Elizabeth and her reputation. We have not changed or simplified these quotations – now that you have studied Elizabeth's reign you will understand what the historians are saying. If there is a word you do not know – ask your teacher!

HISTORIANS ON ELIZABETH

Read each of the following extracts and then identify the main points each historian is making particularly their assessment of Elizabeth's reputation.

Extract A 'Elizabeth I' by S. Doran, *The Historian*, No. 54, 1997

Elizabeth's political aims and style of government were more complex than her image-makers and admirers have admitted. In addition, her popularity and solidarity with her subjects can no longer be taken for granted, especially during the last decade of her reign. Nonetheless, her achievements as a ruler should not be underestimated. Despite enormous difficulties and several major crises, she survived as monarch with her Protestant religious settlement intact, while her realm was preserved from successful invasion and the civil war which afflicted her neighbours, Scotland, France and the Netherlands. Fifteen years of warfare created stresses certainly, but not the financial collapse or large scale political unrest which often comes in the wake of war. This stability and security owed much to Elizabeth's firm but flexible leadership, and her conservative and relatively cautious policies. What more could be expected of a sixteenth century ruler?

Extract B *Elizabeth I* by C. Haigh, 1988

Elizabeth died unloved and it was partly her own fault. She ended her days as an irascible old woman, presiding over war and failure abroad and poverty and factionalism [divisions] at home. Her reign had been thirty years of illusions, followed by fifteen of disillusion. The English never loved the real Elizabeth; they loved the image she had created.

Extract C *The Elizabethan Nation* by J. Hurstfield, 1964

She tried hard to heal the wounds and divisions of the England she inherited, and she met with a large measure of success ... In her public tasks she succeeded admirably during the first thirty years of her reign in healing the wounds and binding the nation to her own purposes; but she failed significantly during the last fifteen. Delay, ambiguity, the elevation of the monarchy to raise the aims and unify the purpose of the Elizabethan people were no longer enough. In one sense her reign was both too long and too short. If she had lived ten years less she might have gone down in history as the most successful monarch to sit on the English throne.

Extract D 'Elizabeth I: Golden Reign of Gloriana' by D. Loades, *The National Archives*, 2003

When Elizabeth died on 24 March 1603, the lamentations [expressions of grief] were theatrical, but there were also sighs of relief – she had become a very difficult old lady. However, the relative failure of her successors magnified her reputation, and she became good Queen Bess, the ever-victorious. No one had quite thought that at the time, in spite of her triumphalist image, but distance lends enchantment to the view. Ultimately, it was to be the use of Elizabethan imagery by the Victorian pioneers of the British Empire which settled the legend in its recent form. Legends are powerful and facts in themselves, but it is the business of the historian to try to establish the reality.

You might read the last sentence of Extract D and despair. When historians themselves cannot agree, what chance is there for the rest of us? However, if you look again at these four very different sources you will see that all or most of them agree on the following:

- The image of Gloriana and a Golden Age exaggerated by Elizabeth and highlighted by the Victorians was never accurate.
- The achievements of the reign all came in the first 30 years.
- The last fifteen years of the reign were disastrous.
- Elizabeth's popularity with her subjects varied and was not as great as her government liked to show.

Modern historians writing since the 1960s, in an age when the concepts of empire and even monarchy are under attack, tend to be more critical of Elizabeth and to challenge the 'Good Queen Bess' image, yet she continues to attract our interest.

If Elizabeth was not Gloriana, then how successful a queen was she? Historian David Loades describes her as:

> ...not the greatest English monarch. In terms of achievement she was probably inferior to Henry II, Edward III, Henry VII, or even Charles II. But she was one of the greatest.

There were certainly achievements, from the establishment of the Church of England to the defeat of the Spanish Armada. That list of problems facing Elizabeth in 1558 (see page 16) had been tackled. The England of 1588 was very different to the one the young Queen had inherited. You have just studied how Elizabeth tried to solve all those problems, and in the final activity on the next page you will have a last opportunity to analyse how well you think she did.

Although definitely no goddess, Elizabeth gave her people a security, pride and sense of purpose which can be found as much in the growth of schools and plays of Shakespeare as in the heroic exploits of Francis Drake. She could not improve the quality of life for all her subjects, but in 1601, the Elizabethan Poor Law made her government accept for the first time that it had a duty to look after those facing real hardship. Above all, and this is perhaps the real reason for her continuing appeal, she did this, against all the odds, as a single woman in a world that was totally dominated by men. She remains the only unmarried queen ever to have ruled England, and so 'the legend' continues.

◀ Elizabeth remains a popular subject for films and TV programmes, as this picture from *Shakespeare in Love* shows. Can you find any others?

8.3 Elizabeth's greatness – what do you think?

Do you think that Elizabeth deserves her reputation as a highly successful Queen who had a glorious reign? Or do you think that she was very lucky to survive and keep her throne because she made so many mistakes? Perhaps you are somewhere in between, and think she did really well in some areas but was a disaster in others? This final activity will give you the opportunity to reach an overall assessment. By analysing the main issues of the reign, you can decide whether the way Elizabeth dealt with them merits her reputation as 'Gloriana'.

Elizabeth was a highly successful queen who had a glorious reign.	Elizabeth was a competent monarch and her reign was fairly successful.	This event does not tell us anything either way.

The challenge from the Catholics

Both in England and Europe, including the role of the Papacy.

Elizabeth's legitimacy, gender and single status

In the sixteenth century, people believed that a successful monarch needed to have adult children to continue the royal family and avoid disputes over the succession.

The problem of Mary, Queen of Scots

The Revolt of the Northern Earls

Successful monarchs were supposed to rule a peaceful and prosperous country, free from plots and rebellions.

Settling religious divisions

Rulers at the time believed their country had to be united behind one religion; any differences could lead to civil war.

The threat from France

France had close links with Scotland, and the legacy of Mary I's reign meant England had just lost the last military base in France.

Plots against the Queen

The Ridolfi, Throckmorton and Babington plots, and the role of Mary, Queen of Scots.

The challenge from the Puritans

Assessing Elizabeth

In pairs or a small group, discuss each of the main issues of the reign described on each of the cards on these pages, and then decide where to place it on the continuum. Some of the cards have extra prompts to remind you of the extent of the problem and why it was important in reaching a verdict on Elizabeth's rule.

When you have placed all your cards on the continuum, you should be able to reach a verdict on Elizabeth's reign and the popular image of Elizabeth as a highly successful monarch. You should now prepare a presentation to explain how you have come to this conclusion.

This event does not tell us anything either way.	Elizabeth just scraped by; her reign had a few successes.	Elizabeth was very lucky to keep her throne; she made so many mistakes.

The defeat of the Spanish Armada, 1588

Privateering in the New World

The impact on relations with Spain, as well as the royal finances.

The growth of education and leisure

Including the theatre.

English intervention in the Netherlands

The impact on relations with Spain.

The increase in poverty and vagabondage

People expected their monarch to ensure that everyone was better-off and provide prosperity and work for all.

War with Spain, 1585–8

Successful monarchs were expected to rule powerful countries with a strong army and navy, to keep their subjects safe from attacks or invasions, and to win any wars.

The establishment of a good government

Successful monarchs needed to keep power in their own hands, while keeping nobles loyal and under control. They needed to choose a Council that would suggest and enforce successful policies.

Exploration and voyages of discovery

Introducing the exam

Simply knowing a lot of content is not enough to achieve a good grade in your GCSE History exam. You need to know how to write effective answers to the questions. Pages 116–121 give you an insight into the exam and provide guidance on how to approach the different questions. This page introduces the structure of Section B (the British depth study) of your Paper 2 exam. The guidance opposite helps you to approach your exam with confidence. Paper 2 is divided into two sections. Section A covers the **period study**. Section B covers the **British depth study**, where you will select: **Option B4: Early Elizabethan England, 1558–88**

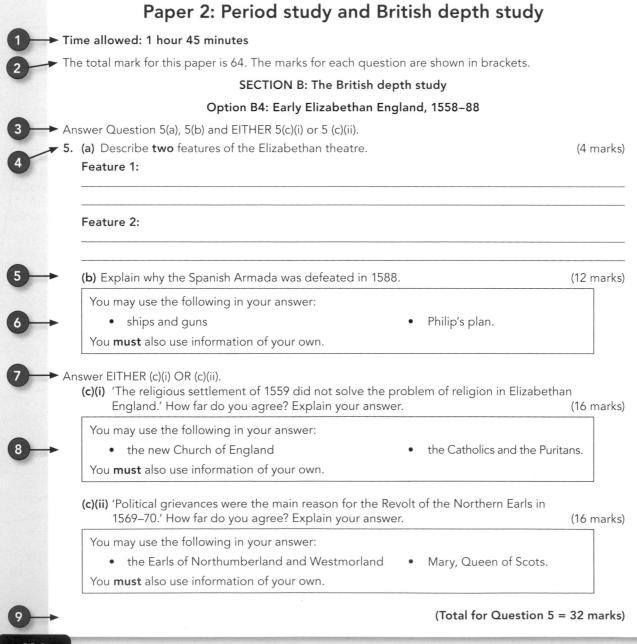

Paper 2: Period study and British depth study

(1) **Time allowed: 1 hour 45 minutes**

(2) The total mark for this paper is 64. The marks for each question are shown in brackets.

SECTION B: The British depth study

Option B4: Early Elizabethan England, 1558–88

(3) Answer Question 5(a), 5(b) and EITHER 5(c)(i) or 5 (c)(ii).

(4) 5. **(a)** Describe **two** features of the Elizabethan theatre. (4 marks)

Feature 1:

_____

_____

Feature 2:

_____

_____

(5) **(b)** Explain why the Spanish Armada was defeated in 1588. (12 marks)

(6)
You may use the following in your answer:
- ships and guns
- Philip's plan.

You **must** also use information of your own.

(7) Answer EITHER (c)(i) OR (c)(ii).

(c)(i) 'The religious settlement of 1559 did not solve the problem of religion in Elizabethan England.' How far do you agree? Explain your answer. (16 marks)

(8)
You may use the following in your answer:
- the new Church of England
- the Catholics and the Puritans.

You **must** also use information of your own.

(c)(ii) 'Political grievances were the main reason for the Revolt of the Northern Earls in 1569–70.' How far do you agree? Explain your answer. (16 marks)

You may use the following in your answer:
- the Earls of Northumberland and Westmorland
- Mary, Queen of Scots.

You **must** also use information of your own.

(9) **(Total for Question 5 = 32 marks)**

Planning for success

1 TIMING

It is important to time yourself carefully. One hour and 45 minutes sounds a long time, but it goes very quickly! Section A (period study) and Section B (British depth study) are worth the same amount of marks. You should aim to spend the same amount of time on each section. For both the period study and the British depth study, it is important to have a time plan and to stick to it.

Look at the plan below. You could use this plan or develop your own and check it with your teacher. We have broken down the depth study into two 25-minute blocks of time. This is because some students spend too long on Questions 5(a) and 5(b). They then rush Question 5(c). However, the final question is worth the same amount of marks as 5(a) and 5(b) put together.

Section A (period study) Questions 1, 2 and 3: approx. 50 minutes

Section B (British depth study on Early Elizabethan England, 1558–88)

Question 5: approx. 50 minutes

Questions 5(a) and 5(b): approx. 25 minutes

EITHER Question 5(c)(i) OR 5(c)(ii): approx. 25 minutes

Checking your answers: 5 minutes

2 SPEND TIME DE-CODING QUESTIONS

The marks for each question are shown in brackets. This gives you an idea of how much you need to write, as does the space for your answer on the exam paper. However, do not panic if you do not fill all the space. There will probably be more space than you need and the quality of your answer is more important than how much you write. The most important thing is to keep focused on the question. If you include information that is not relevant to the question, you will not gain any marks, no matter how much you write!

Read each question carefully before you to start to answer it. Use the advice on de-coding questions on page 116 to make sure you focus on the question.

3 FOLLOW INSTRUCTIONS CAREFULLY

Read the instructions very carefully. Some students miss questions they need to answer, while others waste time answering more questions than they need to. Remember to answer Question 5(a) AND 5(b). You then need to choose between EITHER Question 5(c)(i) OR 5(c)(ii).

4 THE 'DESCRIBE' QUESTION

The first question on Section B asks you to describe two features of an aspect of the period you have studied. Headings on the exam paper help you to write about each feature separately. Advice on how to gain high marks on this type of question is on page 117.

5 THE 'EXPLAIN' QUESTION

The second question tests your ability to write effective explanations. You may be asked to explain why an event or development took place. Pages 118–119 helps you to write a good answer to this type of question.

6 USING THE STIMULUS MATERIAL

When you attempt Question 5(b) and either Question 5(c)(i) or (c)(ii), you will have bullet points as stimulus material to help plan your answer. You do not have to include them, but try to use them to get you thinking and to support your arguments. You must bring in your own knowledge too. If you only use the stimulus material, you will not gain high marks for your answer.

7 THINK CAREFULLY ABOUT WHICH QUESTION YOU CHOOSE

When it comes to the choice of final question, do not rush your decision. Think carefully about which question you will perform best on. Plan your answer – it is worth 16 marks, half the available marks for Section B of the exam paper.

8 THE 'JUDGEMENT' QUESTION

This question carries the most marks and requires a longer answer that needs careful planning. You will be provided with a statement and you have to reach a judgement as to how far you agree with that statement. Pages 120–1 provide advice on answering this style of question.

REMEMBER

Checking the quality of your writing

Make sure you leave five minutes at the end of the exam to check your answers. If you are short of time, check your answer to the final question first, as it carries the most marks. Page 121 provides advice on what to focus on. Remember that the accuracy of your spelling, punctuation and grammar is important in all questions, as it affects the clarity of your answer.

De-coding exam questions

The examiners are not trying to catch you out: they are giving you a chance to show what you know – and what you can do with what you know. However, you must stick to the question on the exam paper. Staying focused on the question is crucial. Including information that is not relevant, or misreading a question and writing about the wrong topic wastes time and gains you no marks.

To stay focused on the question, you will need to practise how to 'decode' questions. This is particularly important for Section B of the exam paper. Follow these **five steps to success**:

Step 1 Read the question a couple of times. Then look at **how many marks** the question is worth. This tells you how much you are expected to write. Do not spend too long on questions only worth a few marks. Remember, it is worth planning the 12- and 16-mark questions.

Step 2 Identify the **conceptual focus** of the question. What is the key concept that the question focuses on? Is it asking you to look at:

- the **significance** of a discovery or individual?
- **causation** – the reasons why an event or development happened?
- **consequence** – the results of an event or development?
- **similarities and differences** – between the key features of different periods?
- **change** – the extent of change or continuity, progress or stagnation during a period?

Step 3 Spot the **question type**. Are you being asked to:

- **describe** – the key features of a period?
- **explain** – similarities between periods or why something happened?
- reach a **judgement** – as to how far you agree with a particular statement?

Each question type requires a different approach. Look for key words or phrases that help you to work out which approach is needed. The phrase 'How far do you agree?' means you need to weigh the evidence for and against a statement before reaching a balanced judgement. 'Explain why' means that you need to explore a range of reasons why an event happened.

Step 4 Identify the **content focus**. What is the area of content or topic the examiner wants you to focus on?

Step 5 Look carefully at the **date boundaries** of the question. What time period should you cover in your answer? Stick to this carefully or you will waste time writing about events that are not relevant to the question.

Look at the exam question below. At first glance, it could appear that this question is only about the political causes of the Revolt of the Northern Earls. This shows the danger of not decoding a question carefully. If you simply describe how political grievances led to the outbreak of the Revolt, you will be missing the main focus of the question. If you explain why these grievances resulted in rebellion, you would gain a few more marks, but you are still not focusing on the actual question.

The content focus is more than just the Earls' political grievances. It is exploring a wider theme – the reasons for the Revolt of the Northern Earls in 1569–70.

The conceptual focus is causation – you need to reach a judgement on whether political grievances were the main cause of the Revolt of the Northern Earls.

> **5(c)(ii)** 'Political grievances were the main reason for the Revolt of the Northern Earls in 1569–70.' How far do you agree? Explain your answer.
>
> (16)

There are 16 marks available – this means the question requires an extended answer. It is definitely worth planning your answer to this question!

The dates provided for the rebellion are important. If you include references to plots and challenges against the Queen after 1570, you will waste time and not pick up any additional marks.

The phrase 'How far do you agree' means that this question requires you to reach a judgement about the statement in quotation marks. This means analysing the impact of the nobles' political grievances in the lead-up to the revolt. It also means weighing the importance of this cause of the revolt against other important causes (such as the arrival of Mary, Queen of Scots).

Further practice

Look at the other questions in Section B of the exam paper on page 114.

Break down each question into the five steps above and check you have decoded the question effectively.

Describing key features of a period

'Describe' questions only carry 4 marks, so it is important to get to the point quickly, so you do not waste precious time needed for questions that carry 12 or 16 marks.

Look at the question below.

> Describe **two** features of the Elizabethan theatre. (4)
>
> Feature 1: _____
>
> Feature 2: _____

Tip 1: stay relevant to the question

One major problem with 'Describe' questions is that students write too much! They include details that are not relevant to the question. Make sure you stick to the question – describe two key features of the Elizabethan theatre.

You do not need to:

- include more than two features (extra features will not gain you any more marks)
- evaluate and reach a judgement
- go beyond any date boundaries.

If you write too much, you could run out of time later in the exam when you are answering questions that are worth a lot more marks and need longer answers.

Tip 2: keep it short and simple

You can get two marks by simply identifying two features of the Elizabethan theatre.

For each feature you identify, add a sentence that adds further detail and develops your answer.

Look at the example below. Then practise your technique by tackling the examples in the practice question box.

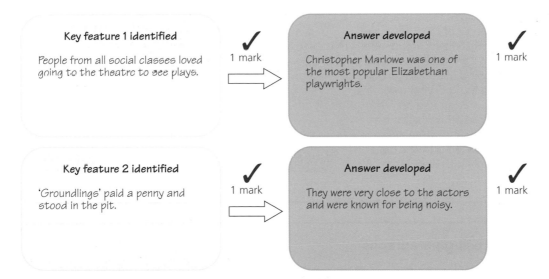

Key feature 1 identified

People from all social classes loved going to the theatre to see plays.

✓ 1 mark

Answer developed

Christopher Marlowe was one of the most popular Elizabethan playwrights.

✓ 1 mark

Key feature 2 identified

'Groundlings' paid a penny and stood in the pit.

✓ 1 mark

Answer developed

They were very close to the actors and were known for being noisy.

✓ 1 mark

Practice questions

1. Describe two features of the Elizabethan Religious Settlement of 1559.
2. Describe two features of Elizabeth's Privy Council.
3. Describe two features of the challenge from the Puritans between 1558 and 1569.
4. Describe two features of the plots against Elizabeth between 1571 and 1587.
5. Describe two features of Elizabethan schools.

REMEMBER

Stay focused and keep it short and simple. Four sentences are enough for four marks.

Tackling 12-mark explain questions

Look at the question below.

> **5(b) Explain why the Spanish Armada was defeated In 1588. (12 marks)**
>
> You may use the following in your answer:
> - ships and guns
> - Philip's plan.
>
> You **must** also use information of your own.

The conceptual focus is on causation (explaining **why** something happened). The question is worth 12 marks. The examiner will expect you to give a range of reasons **why** the Spanish Armada was defeated in 1588.

It is important to spend time planning this question during your exam. Follow the steps below to help you plan effectively and produce a good answer.

Step 1: Get focused on the question

Make sure you decode the question carefully. Note that the content focus is on the defeat of the Armada and the date boundary is 'in 1588'. Do not go into the causes of the Spanish Armada or why Spain and England were at war.

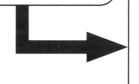

Step 2: Identify a range of factors

Try to cover more than one cause (as shown in the diagram below). If your mind goes blank, the stimulus bullet points can help you. For example, in the question above, 'ships and guns' should make you remember to analyse the size and features of the English and Spanish fleets. Remember – you are expected to go beyond the bullet points and bring in your own knowledge – so do not be put off if a factor that you want to write about is not covered by the bullet points provided.

Step 3: Organise your answer using paragraphs

Do not worry about writing a long introduction. One or two sentences are more than enough and you can use words from the question. Look at the example below. Note how the student has built a short introduction into the first paragraph which focuses on the importance of the defeat and a possible reason for it.

> *The defeat of the Spanish Armada was one of the great English naval victories. Spain was the most powerful empire in Europe at the time and her fleet would have been expected to win. However, the weather played an important role in the defeat of the Spanish Armada. This is because...*

Aim to start a new paragraph each time you move on to a new factor that caused the defeat. Signpost your argument at the start of the paragraph. For example, you could start your next paragraph like this:

> *This popular view of the importance of the weather in explaining the Armada's defeat is accurate, but there were other reasons too. To start with, Philip's plan and instructions to his fleet were very ambitious.*

Step 4: Do not 'say' that a factor was important – 'prove' it was

Remember that a list of reasons for the defeat of the Spanish Armada will not get you a high-level mark. You need to **prove** your case for each factor. This means developing your explanation by adding supporting information and specific examples (killer evidence).

This is where your work on connectives will come in useful. Look again at the advice on page 58, and remember to tie what you know to the question by using connectives such as 'this meant that …', 'this led to …' and 'this resulted in …'. For example, you may want to build on the opening to your second paragraph by proving that Philip's plan was a key reason for the Armada's defeat.

> Philip's plan depended on reaching and controlling a Channel port, rendezvousing with Parma's army and then ferrying 20,000 soldiers across to England on barges. In an age of poor communication with transport subject to the weather, the ambitious nature of the plan meant that it was highly likely that it would go wrong. In the event, Parma's army was delayed by Dutch rebels and Philip's fleet was chased from Calais by English fireships. Philip's plan, therefore, contributed to the defeat of the Spanish Armada.

WHAT YOU KNOW — WHAT THE QUESTION ASKS

Practice questions

You can find further practice questions on pages 29, 59 and 74.

REMEMBER

Do not try to cover too many reasons for an event. Select which causes you can make the strongest argument for. Remember in the exam you would have approximately 15 minutes to answer this question.

Step 5: end your answer with a thoughtful conclusion

Keep your conclusion short. A good conclusion makes the overall argument clear – it is not a detailed summary of everything you have already written! Make it clear which factor played the most important role. You may want to show how it links to other factors.

Advice	Model
Start by showing that you are aware that a range of factors played a role.	There was more than one reason for the defeat of the Armada. Philip's plan was highly ambitious and did not allow for any problems, such as those caused by the bad weather, in particular the winds. Other reasons, such as the quality of leadership, the tactics used and the resources of the two sides are more balanced on paper, but once the fighting started, in all these areas the English proved to have the edge over the Spanish.
Make it clear which factor you think played the most important role.	Ultimately, it was the weather and the change in the direction of the wind that brought about the defeat of the Armada. It also exposed the weaknesses in Philip's plan and the limited quality of the Spanish leadership, which was unable to respond to this.
Support your argument with the key reason why you have come to this conclusion.	Using the stiff breeze to send in the fireships caused panic and the breaking of the Spanish fleet's formation, which allowed the faster, small English ships to get in close and inflict severe damage with their continually firing guns. The end came when the winds blew the now anchorless Spanish ships north, where storms drove many of them onto the coasts of Scotland and Ireland, with considerable loss of life.

Making judgements – tackling the 16-mark question

The last question on the exam paper carries the most marks and requires a carefully planned, detailed answer. You will be provided with a statement in quotation marks and asked to reach a judgement about **how far you agree** with it. The phrase 'how far' is important, as it is unlikely that you will totally agree or disagree with the statement. The examiner will be looking for you to show that you can weigh the evidence for and against the statement.

Look at the example below.

> **(c)(i)** 'The Religious Settlement of 1559 did not solve the problem of religion in Elizabethan England.' How far do you agree? Explain your answer. (16)
>
> You may use the following in your answer:
> - the new Church of England
> - the Catholics and the Puritans.
>
> You **must** also use information of your own.

Follow the same steps that you would for an 'explain' question (see pages 118–119).

Step 1: Focus

The content focus is important – you have to reach a judgement on the main consequences of Elizabeth's Religious Settlement. The conceptual focus is on consequences. Focus on the phrase 'did not solve' in the question – what problems was the Religious Settlement supposed to solve, and did it make them better or worse?

Think of what Elizabeth was trying to do in the Religious Settlement and what she managed to achieve.

Think of the consequences of the Religious Settlement. How did different people react to it? Had she solved some or all of the problems? What were the consequences for the Queen and the country?

Step 2: Identify

The 16-mark questions require you to reach a judgement on a statement. In order to do this effectively, you need to identify **clear criteria** for reaching that judgement. Just like you need to cover a range of factors in 'explain' questions, you need to **cover a range of criteria** in 'judgement' questions.

Possible criteria for reaching a judgement:

- You could evaluate different sorts of consequences as your criteria by looking at short and long term consequences. Did the settlement create initial problems but over time opposition decreased?
- You could also analyse how many people were affected by the event. Did the majority of people accept the new Church? Was it only opposed by a few and, if so, how important were they?

Step 3: Organise

The simplest way to plan for judgement-style questions is to think in terms of 'for' and 'against' paragraphs:

Paragraph 1 Evidence to **support** the statement. For example, show how there was opposition to the new Church from both Catholics and Puritans for the rest of the reign.

Paragraph 2 Evidence to **counter** the statement. Show how the Religious Settlement did not please everyone, but was enough of a compromise between Catholicism and Puritanism to be acceptable to most people.

Paragraph 3 Your final conclusion – weigh the evidence. How far do you agree with the statement?

Step 4: Prove

Remember to tie what you know to the question. Do not include information and think that it will speak for itself. Some students think that simply dropping in examples to the right paragraphs is enough. The following statement from a student could be further developed and gain more marks.

> Another important consequence of the Religious Settlement was that Elizabeth was now Supreme Governor of the Church of England.

This does not **prove** that the Religious Settlement had important consequences. The student needs to go on to explain how Elizabeth's appointment as Supreme Governor alienated many Catholics and meant they could not accept the Settlement because they believed only the Pope could be Head of the Church. In other words, this links back to the main theme of not solving all the problems (for all the people).

Step 5: Conclude

Your conclusion is a crucial part of your answer. You have been asked to reach a judgement on a statement. You need to state clearly how far you agree with it and your reasons why. It would be easy to sit on the fence and avoid reaching a final conclusion. But sitting on the fence is a dangerous position. Your answer collapses and you lose marks.

Instead of sitting on the fence, you need to be confident and reach an overall judgement. Imagine that you have placed the evidence on a set of scales.

How far do they tip in favour of the statement or against it? If they are in position 1, you might conclude that you agree with the statement 'to a large extent'; for position 2, 'to some extent', while for position 3, you might conclude that you 'mainly disagree' with the statement.

You can then move on in your conclusion to explain your judgement. Do not repeat everything you have already written. Think of the scales – what are the heaviest pieces of evidence on each side? Build these into your conclusion in the following way:

JUDGEMENT – Start with your judgement – try to incorporate words from the question into this sentence.	To a large extent, I agree that Elizabeth's Religious Settlement of 1559 did not solve the problem of religion in England.
COUNTER – Show that you are aware that there is some evidence to counter this, and give the best example.	However, the new Church of England was acceptable to many people. It combined the appearance of the Catholic Church with Protestant doctrine and was enforced in a way that did not make martyrs of opponents.
SUPPORT – Explain why, overall, you have reached your judgement. Give your key reason or reasons why.	The Religious Settlement did not solve all the problems of religion. However, given the importance of religion and the fact that people were prepared to die for their religious differences, it was unlikely that any settlement would have been able to do this. It was as good a settlement as could have been achieved at the time, and by the end of the reign, with the problems of both the Catholics and the Puritans greatly reduced, it was regarded as one of Elizabeth's successes.

Practice questions

You can find further practice questions on pages 29, 59 and 94.

REMEMBER

Leave enough time to **check your answer** carefully for spelling, punctuation and grammar.

- Is your spelling and punctuation accurate?
- Does your work make sense? Are your arguments clear?
- Have you used a wide range of historical terms?

What are the key ingredients of effective writing in GCSE history?

The language you use to express your ideas is very important. One of the ways to get better at History is to be more precise with your use of language. For example, rather than simply saying that you **agree** or **disagree** with a statement, you can use language that shows whether you agree to **a large extent** or only **to some extent**. Look at the different shades of argument below and experiment with using some of the phrases. Use them when you are debating or discussing in class.

Strong language

Tentative language

Thinking carefully about the language you use

Varying your language to show how far you agree with a statement:

I totally/entirely/completely/absolutely agree with …

I substantially/fundamentally/strongly agree with …

I agree to a large extent with … I mainly/mostly agree with …

I agree to some extent with … I partially/partly agree with …

I only agree with … to a limited/slight extent.

Varying your language to show how important a factor/cause is:

… was by far the most important reason why …

The key/crucial/essential factor was …

… was the main cause of … The most influential cause was …

… played a significant/important/major role in …

… was of some importance in …

Varying your language to show the significance or importance of an individual, discovery, event or development:

… made the most important/significant contribution to …

… had a crucial/major/highly significant impact on …

… had an important/influential impact on …

… was of some importance/significance

… only made a limited/partial/slight/minimal contribution to …

Varying your language to show the extent of change:

… was revolutionised in … / … totally changed during …

… was transformed during … /
,… there was fundamental change in …

The period saw significant/important progress in …

… saw some changes/progress in …

… saw limited/slight/minimal progress in …

Helpful phrases and sentence starters		
When you want to explore the other side of an argument:	**When you want to highlight similarities:**	**When you want to make an additional point to support an argument:**
On the other hand …	In the same way …	Also … Additionally … In addition …
However …	Similarly … This is similar to the way that …	Moreover …
Alternatively, it could be argued that …	Likewise …	Furthermore …
When you want to link points or show that one thing led to another:	**When you want to give examples to support a point:**	**When you want to show that an individual, event or discovery was important:**
Therefore … Due to …	For example … For instance …	… was a crucial turning point in …
Consequently … One consequence of this was …	This can be seen when … This is clearly shown by …	… acted as an important catalyst for …
This caused … This led to … This resulted in … This meant that …	This is supported by … This is proven by …	Without this event/development/discovery … would not have happened.
		This had an immediate impact on …
		In the short term, this transformed/revolutionised …
		In the long term, this had a lasting impact on …

Self-assessing and peer-assessing your work

It is important that you check your own work before you hand it to your teacher to be marked. Sometimes you may be asked to assess the work of someone else in your class. In both cases, you need to know what you are looking for.

What are the key ingredients of great writing in History? You can use the **bingo card** as a checklist – get competitive and try to show that you have covered all the squares and got a full house of ingredients!

The answer starts with a **clear focus on the question** (there is no long introduction). Key words from the question are used during the answer. For longer answers, each paragraph is linked to the question.	Statements and arguments are fully developed and explained – showing good knowledge and understanding. Arguments are **well supported** by accurate, relevant and well-selected evidence.	**Connectives** are used to help prove arguments and show significance/impact. Look for phrases like: *this led to …* *this resulted in …* *this meant that …*
There is a **clear line of argument** at the start of each paragraph – think of it as a signpost for what follows. The rest of the paragraph supports this argument. The line of argument flows throughout the answer, building up to a clear conclusion.	Paragraphs have been used to provide a **clear structure**. Each paragraph starts with • a different cause/factor (12-mark 'explain' questions) or • a different theme/criteria (16-mark 'judgement' questions).	The answers shows **wide-ranging** knowledge and understanding. It considers a range of factors/causes ('explain' questions) or explores the evidence for **and** against a statement ('judgement' questions).
The language used helps to construct very precise arguments – showing how important the writer thinks a cause/factor, event or individual is. A good range of specialist **historical vocabulary** has been used.	There is a **clear conclusion**. For 'explain' questions, factors/causes are prioritised or linked. For 'judgement' questions, there is a focus on 'how far' the writer agrees with the statement.	The answer has been **carefully checked** for spelling, punctuation and grammar. The meaning is always clear throughout the answer.

You can use the **progression grid** below to get an idea of what getting better at History looks like. This is designed to give you a general idea of what you need to do to produce good answers in the exam. It focuses on the four key things in the coloured squares on the bingo card.

The History progression grid

	Question focus	Organisation	Line of argument	Supporting information
High level	The answer is consistently focused on the question.	The answer is structured very carefully and explanations are coherent throughout the answer.	The line of argument is very clear and convincing. It flows throughout the answer.	Supporting information has been precisely selected and shows wide-ranging knowledge and understanding.
	The answer is mainly focused on the question.	The answer is well organised, but some parts of the answer lack coherence.	The line of argument is clear, convincing and generally maintained through the answer.	Supporting information is accurate and relevant, and shows good knowledge and understanding.
	The answer has weak or limited links to the question.	Some statements are developed and there is some attempt to organise the material.	The line of argument is partly convincing, but not maintained through the answer.	Supporting information is mainly accurate and relevant, and shows some knowledge and understanding.
	The answer has no real links to the question.	The answer lacks organisation.	The line of argument is unclear or missing.	Supporting information is limited or not relevant.

Glossary

Abdicate   To give up or renounce one's position, especially as monarch.

Accession Day   The anniversary of the date on which a monarch takes the throne.

Ambassador   An official envoy representing a state or country.

Armada   Spanish word meaning a naval fleet or group of warships.

Astrolabe   An instrument used by sailors to calculate their position by the stars.

Aztecs   Tribes living in central Mexico between the fourteenth and sixteenth centuries, and one of the last great Native American civilisations.

Bark   A small ship with three masts.

Black comedy   Comedy which uses farce or morbid humour, often joking about subjects that are delicate or taboo.

Bullion   Bars of gold and silver, such as those being shipped to the Spanish Netherlands.

Chaplain   A religious minister attached to a secular institution, particularly the military.

Civil war   Armed conflict between two opposite sides in the same country.

Clergy   People who have been trained and approved for carrying out religious services in the Church, for example, priests.

Colonists   People who have settled in a colony.

Colony   A country under full or partial control of another, and occupied by settlers from that country.

Commissioner   An official appointed, usually by the crown, to undertake a specific function in connection with the enforcement of the law.

Comptroller   In charge of the accounts in government finance departments.

Court   The community of people who lived with the Queen, including advisers, officials, ladies-in-waiting and servants.

Crucifixes   Images of Jesus on the cross.

Customs duties   Taxes paid to the government on goods coming into the country (imports).

Dissolution of the Monasteries   The administrative and legal processes between 1536 and 1541 by which Henry VIII disbanded the Catholic monasteries and appropriated their wealth.

Doctrine   The teachings and beliefs of the Church.

Dynasty   A succession of generations from a ruling family.

Exchequer   The government department which looked after the crown's finances.

Excommunicate   To be excommunicated meant you were no longer a member of the Catholic Church. This gave Elizabeth's enemies justification for rebelling and replacing her with a Catholic.

Feudal dues   Money paid to the monarch as a landowner by his tenants-in-chief to mark traditions, such as tenant's heir coming of age (21st birthday).

Flyboat   A small, fast, sailing boat.

Galleon   A large sailing ship with several decks, used in Spain between the fifteenth and eighteenth centuries, originally as a warship, and later for trade.

Garrison   A body of troops stationed in a fortified place.

Gloriana   A name given to Elizabeth I because she was so gloriously successful and majestic, even godlike.

Governor General   Ruler of the Netherlands in the sixteenth century, in the absence of the monarch.

Gunpowder Plot   The failed assassination attempt against King James I in 1605, by provincial English Catholics, including Guy Fawkes.

Heathen   A person who does not belong to a religion.

Heretic   Someone whose religious beliefs go against the teachings of the Church.

Holy Communion   Also known as Eucharist – a religious rite in which wine and bread, representing the blood and body of Christ, are tasted by the congregation.

Holy days   Days on which the Catholic Church requires the faithful to participate in a Mass.

Holy Roman Emperor   Ruler elected, usually from the Habsburg family, to govern territories in central Europe, including Austria and Germany.

Inca   A member of the South American people who established an empire in Peru before the Spanish conquest.

Inflammable   Easily set on fire.

Jesuit   Catholic missionary priest, whose aim was to convert or re-convert countries to Catholicism and the authority of the Pope.

Justices of the Peace (JPs)   Appointed by the monarch, usually from the gentry class, to keep law and order in their district and carry out the orders of the Privy Council.

Last Judgement   The second coming of Christ and the final and eternal judgement of all humanity by God.

Latitude   Imaginary lines circling the globe horizontally, to the north and south of the Equator and parallel to it, used (in conjunction with imaginary lines of longitude) by mapmakers and navigators to record and locate places.

Longitude   As for 'Latitude', but with parallel lines running vertically from north to south.

Lord High Admiral   Appointed by the monarch to take control of all navy operations.

Lord Lieutenants   Responsible for governing each county for the crown and organising the local militia or army.

Lord Treasurer   Member of the Privy Council in charge of the country's finances.

Madrigal   A non-religious song, usually for between two and eight voices.

Maritime empire   The dominant power controlling its territories through seas and oceans and with ships.

Martyr   A person who is killed because of his or her religious beliefs.

Masques   Lavish and extravagant court entertainments where famous events were shown through dance and mime.

Mass   The name given to the Communion Service by Catholics where the priest spoke in Latin and communicants believed the bread and wine were transformed into the body and blood of Jesus.

Miniature   A very small painting, especially a portrait.

Missionary   A person sent on a religious mission to promote their religion in a foreign country.

Monopoly   A royal licence which gave individuals the sole right to manufacture or sell a product. The individual paid the Queen for the licence so her government made money, but the people believed monopolies led to an increase in prices.

Mutiny   An open rebellion against the proper authorities, especially by soldiers or sailors.

New World   A sixteenth-century name for North and South America, especially during its exploration and colonisation by Europeans.

Page   A man or boy employed as an attendant of a person of rank.

Parliament   Parliament was summoned by the Queen when she needed laws passed or taxes raised. Members of the House of Commons were nominated by the crown or a noble, and all nobles sat in the House of Lords.

Pinnace   A small ship with oars and sails.

Piracy   The practice of attacking and robbing ships at sea.

Privy Council   The committee of minsters appointed by Elizabeth to advise her.

Propaganda   Materials issued, usually by governments, to persuade people to think or behave in a certain way.

Protestant Reformation   A Christian movement in sixteenth-century Europe which broke away from Catholicism and the authority of the Pope.

Puritans   A term applied to a variety of English Protestants over the centuries. Here it is used in the sense common in Elizabeth's reign of Protestants who wanted to remove all Catholic practices and rituals from the new Church of England and to focus instead on preaching the Scriptures.

Relics   (Alleged) parts of a deceased holy person's body, kept as objects to be revered.

Religious crusade   A holy war with a religious purpose, usually to recapture and convert lands.

Renaissance   The revival of European art and literature under the influence of classical models in the fourteenth to sixteenth centuries.

Requiem Mass   A Catholic service said for the souls of the dead.

Secretary of State   The most important position on the Privy Council; this person supervised all government business, managed meetings of Parliament and was in close contact with the Queen.

State funeral   A public funeral ceremony held to honour people of national significance.

Succession   The act or process of inheriting a title or office, including the English monarchy.

Surplice   A white tunic usually worn by Catholic clergy.

True North   Geographic, not magnetic, north, as determined by the North Star and the North Pole.

Usurper   Someone who wrongfully takes someone else's place, for example, on the throne.

Vagabondage   Vagrancy, homelessness, wandering without a purpose.

Vagabonds   Wandering beggars who often turned to crime. They were seen as a threat to society in the sixteenth century and were treated harshly.

Vatican   The palace of the Pope in Rome, including administrative offices.

Warning beacons   Fires lit at well-known locations on hills or high places, to warn of enemy ships or troops.

Yeomen   Farmers who owned their own land; some yeomen grew quite wealthy during Elizabeth's reign.

Answers to 'Understanding Elizabethan England' activity, page 3:

1. c)	**5.** a) False	e) True
2. b)	b) True	f) False
3. c)	c) True	g) True
4. a)	d) True	

Answers to the 'Armada' portrait questions, page 46:

1.
- ■ Arrival of the Spanish Armada in the Channel
- ■ Defeat of the Spanish Armada
- ■ The extent of Elizabeth's power stretching beyond England – her hand is on the New World
- ■ Symbol of Elizabeth's royalty and majesty

2. The image of an increasingly powerful monarch who has successfully defended her country from invasion.

Index